50 New Years Baking Recipes for Home

By: Kelly Johnson

Table of Contents

- Classic Vanilla Cupcakes
- Chocolate Peppermint Cake
- Cinnamon Roll Wreath
- Gingerbread Cookies
- Champagne Cupcakes
- Red Velvet Cheesecake Brownies
- Pecan Pie Bars
- Raspberry Almond Linzer Cookies
- Lemon Blueberry Bundt Cake
- Eggnog Snickerdoodles
- Salted Caramel Brownies
- Sparkling Lemon Bars
- Mocha Hazelnut Tart
- Apple Cider Donuts
- Cream Cheese Sugar Cookies
- Black Forest Cake
- Maple Walnut Scones
- Mint Chocolate Chip Muffins
- White Chocolate Cranberry Blondies
- Pumpkin Spice Bundt Cake
- Almond Joy Cheesecake
- Tiramisu Cupcakes
- Chocolate Chip Pumpkin Bread
- Vanilla Bean Panna Cotta
- Carrot Cake Whoopie Pies
- Strawberry Shortcake Bars
- Espresso Macarons
- Poppy Seed Lemon Muffins
- Chocolate Dipped Pretzel Rods
- Pear Ginger Cake
- Cinnamon Streusel Coffee Cake
- S'mores Brownies
- Coconut Lime Bars
- Nutella Swirl Banana Bread
- Berry Crumble Bars
- Toffee Pecan Cookies

- Chocolate Raspberry Tart
- Apple Streusel Muffins
- Peanut Butter Cupcakes
- Chai Spice Cake
- Tiramisu Cheesecake
- Hazelnut Mocha Brownies
- Lemon Ricotta Pound Cake
- Gingerbread Bundt Cake
- Peppermint Meringue Cookies
- Chocolate Cherry Cheesecake
- Orange Almond Biscotti
- Caramel Apple Cake
- Strawberry Lemonade Bars
- Bourbon Pecan Pie

Classic Vanilla Cupcakes

Ingredients:

For the Cupcakes:

- 1 1/2 cups (190g) all-purpose flour
- 1 cup (200g) granulated sugar
- 1/2 cup (115g) unsalted butter, room temperature
- 1/2 cup (120ml) milk (whole or 2%)
- 2 large eggs
- 1 1/2 teaspoons vanilla extract
- 1 1/2 teaspoons baking powder
- 1/4 teaspoon salt

For the Frosting:

- 1/2 cup (115g) unsalted butter, room temperature
- 1 1/2 cups (190g) powdered sugar
- 1-2 tablespoons milk
- 1 teaspoon vanilla extract

Instructions:

1. Prepare the Cupcake Batter:

1. Preheat your oven to 350°F (175°C). Line a muffin tin with paper liners.
2. In a medium bowl, whisk together the flour, baking powder, and salt.
3. In a large bowl, beat the butter and sugar together until light and fluffy.
4. Add the eggs one at a time, beating well after each addition. Mix in the vanilla extract.
5. Gradually add the flour mixture to the butter mixture, alternating with the milk, starting and ending with the flour mixture. Mix until just combined.

2. Bake the Cupcakes:

1. Divide the batter evenly among the cupcake liners, filling each about 2/3 full.
2. Bake for 18-20 minutes, or until a toothpick inserted into the center comes out clean.
3. Let the cupcakes cool in the tin for 5 minutes, then transfer them to a wire rack to cool completely.

3. Make the Frosting:

1. Beat the butter until creamy.
2. Gradually add the powdered sugar, beating well after each addition.
3. Add 1 tablespoon of milk and the vanilla extract. Beat until smooth and creamy. If needed, add more milk to reach your desired consistency.

4. Frost the Cupcakes:

1. Once the cupcakes are completely cool, frost them with the vanilla buttercream using a knife or piping bag.

Enjoy your classic vanilla cupcakes!

Chocolate Peppermint Cake

Ingredients:

For the Cake:

- 1 3/4 cups (220g) all-purpose flour
- 1 1/2 cups (300g) granulated sugar
- 3/4 cup (65g) unsweetened cocoa powder
- 1 1/2 teaspoons baking powder
- 1 1/2 teaspoons baking soda
- 1/2 teaspoon salt
- 2 large eggs
- 1 cup (240ml) buttermilk (or milk with 1 tablespoon lemon juice or vinegar)
- 1/2 cup (120ml) vegetable oil
- 2 teaspoons vanilla extract
- 1 cup (240ml) boiling water
- 1/2 cup (120ml) peppermint schnapps or peppermint extract (adjust according to preference)

For the Peppermint Frosting:

- 1 cup (230g) unsalted butter, room temperature
- 3 1/2 cups (440g) powdered sugar
- 1/4 cup (20g) unsweetened cocoa powder
- 1/4 cup (60ml) heavy cream
- 1 teaspoon vanilla extract
- 1/2 teaspoon peppermint extract (or to taste)
- Crushed candy canes or peppermint candies, for garnish

Instructions:

1. Prepare the Cake:

1. Preheat your oven to 350°F (175°C). Grease and flour two 9-inch round cake pans, or line them with parchment paper.
2. In a large bowl, whisk together the flour, sugar, cocoa powder, baking powder, baking soda, and salt.
3. In another bowl, beat the eggs. Add the buttermilk, vegetable oil, vanilla extract, and peppermint schnapps (or extract). Mix well.
4. Gradually add the wet ingredients to the dry ingredients, mixing until just combined.
5. Carefully stir in the boiling water until the batter is smooth (it will be thin).
6. Divide the batter evenly between the prepared pans.
7. Bake for 30-35 minutes, or until a toothpick inserted into the center comes out clean.
8. Allow the cakes to cool in the pans for 10 minutes, then transfer them to a wire rack to cool completely.

2. Make the Peppermint Frosting:

1. Beat the butter in a large bowl until creamy.
2. Gradually add the powdered sugar and cocoa powder, mixing on low speed until combined.
3. Add the heavy cream, vanilla extract, and peppermint extract. Beat on high speed until the frosting is light and fluffy.
4. Adjust the peppermint flavor to taste, adding more extract if needed.

3. Assemble the Cake:

1. Place one cake layer on a serving plate or cake stand. Spread a layer of frosting on top.
2. Place the second cake layer on top of the frosted layer.
3. Frost the top and sides of the cake with the peppermint frosting.
4. Garnish with crushed candy canes or peppermint candies.

Enjoy your festive and flavorful Chocolate Peppermint Cake!

Cinnamon Roll Wreath

Ingredients:

For the Dough:

- 1 cup (240ml) whole milk
- 1/2 cup (115g) unsalted butter
- 1/4 cup (50g) granulated sugar
- 2 1/4 teaspoons (1 packet) active dry yeast
- 1/4 cup (50g) granulated sugar
- 1/2 teaspoon salt
- 2 large eggs
- 4 cups (500g) all-purpose flour

For the Filling:

- 1/2 cup (115g) unsalted butter, softened
- 1 cup (220g) packed brown sugar
- 2 tablespoons ground cinnamon
- 1/4 teaspoon ground nutmeg (optional)

For the Glaze:

- 1 cup (120g) powdered sugar
- 2 tablespoons milk
- 1/2 teaspoon vanilla extract

Instructions:

1. Prepare the Dough:

1. In a small saucepan, heat the milk until warm (about 110°F/45°C). Add the butter and sugar, stirring until the butter is melted and the sugar is dissolved. Let it cool slightly.
2. Sprinkle the yeast over the milk mixture and let it sit for about 5 minutes, or until it becomes frothy.
3. In a large mixing bowl, combine the flour, salt, and 1/4 cup sugar. Make a well in the center and add the yeast mixture and eggs.
4. Mix until a dough forms. Knead on a lightly floured surface for about 5-7 minutes, or until smooth and elastic.
5. Place the dough in a lightly greased bowl, cover with a damp cloth or plastic wrap, and let it rise in a warm place for about 1 hour, or until doubled in size.

2. Prepare the Filling:

1. In a small bowl, combine the brown sugar, cinnamon, and nutmeg (if using).

3. Assemble the Wreath:

1. Preheat your oven to 350°F (175°C). Grease a large baking sheet or line it with parchment paper.
2. Punch down the risen dough and roll it out on a lightly floured surface into a rectangle, about 16x12 inches.
3. Spread the softened butter evenly over the dough.
4. Sprinkle the cinnamon-sugar mixture evenly over the buttered dough.
5. Starting from one long edge, roll up the dough tightly into a log. Pinch the seam to seal.
6. Slice the dough log into 12-15 equal pieces.
7. Arrange the slices in a circle on the prepared baking sheet, overlapping them slightly to form a wreath shape.
8. Cover with a damp cloth and let rise for about 30 minutes, or until puffy.
9. Bake for 25-30 minutes, or until golden brown.

4. Make the Glaze:

1. In a small bowl, whisk together the powdered sugar, milk, and vanilla extract until smooth.

5. Finish the Wreath:

1. Let the cinnamon roll wreath cool slightly on a wire rack.
2. Drizzle the glaze over the warm wreath.

Enjoy your festive and delicious Cinnamon Roll Wreath!

Gingerbread Cookies

Ingredients:

For the Cookies:

- 3 1/4 cups (400g) all-purpose flour
- 1/2 teaspoon baking soda
- 1/2 teaspoon baking powder
- 1 tablespoon ground ginger
- 1 tablespoon ground cinnamon
- 1/2 teaspoon ground cloves
- 1/4 teaspoon ground nutmeg
- 1/4 teaspoon salt
- 1/2 cup (115g) unsalted butter, room temperature
- 1/2 cup (100g) granulated sugar
- 1/2 cup (160g) molasses
- 1 large egg

For the Royal Icing (Optional):

- 2 large egg whites
- 4 cups (480g) powdered sugar
- 1 teaspoon lemon juice (or white vinegar)
- Food coloring (optional)

Instructions:

1. Prepare the Dough:

1. In a medium bowl, whisk together the flour, baking soda, baking powder, ginger, cinnamon, cloves, nutmeg, and salt.
2. In a large bowl, beat the butter and sugar together until light and fluffy.
3. Mix in the molasses and egg until well combined.
4. Gradually add the flour mixture to the butter mixture, mixing until the dough comes together. It will be thick.
5. Divide the dough into two equal portions, flatten each into a disk, and wrap in plastic wrap. Chill in the refrigerator for at least 1 hour, or until firm.

2. Roll and Cut the Cookies:

1. Preheat your oven to 350°F (175°C). Line baking sheets with parchment paper.
2. On a lightly floured surface, roll out one disk of dough to about 1/8-inch thickness.
3. Use cookie cutters to cut out shapes and transfer them to the prepared baking sheets.
4. Re-roll and cut any remaining dough. If desired, use a small round cutter to make holes in the top of the cookies for hanging (if making ornaments).

5. Bake for 8-10 minutes, or until the edges are firm but not darkened. The cookies will harden as they cool.

3. Make the Royal Icing (Optional):

1. In a large bowl, beat the egg whites until frothy.
2. Gradually add the powdered sugar and lemon juice, beating until the mixture forms stiff peaks.
3. If desired, divide the icing into bowls and tint with food coloring.

4. Decorate the Cookies:

1. Once the cookies are completely cooled, use a piping bag or a small brush to apply the royal icing. Decorate with additional edible decorations if desired.
2. Allow the icing to dry completely before storing or handling.

Enjoy your homemade gingerbread cookies!

Champagne Cupcakes

Ingredients:

For the Cupcakes:

- 1 1/2 cups (190g) all-purpose flour
- 1 cup (200g) granulated sugar
- 1 1/2 teaspoons baking powder
- 1/2 teaspoon salt
- 1/2 cup (115g) unsalted butter, room temperature
- 1/2 cup (120ml) Champagne or sparkling wine (chilled)
- 1/4 cup (60ml) milk
- 2 large eggs
- 1 teaspoon vanilla extract

For the Champagne Buttercream Frosting:

- 1 cup (230g) unsalted butter, room temperature
- 3 1/2 cups (440g) powdered sugar
- 2-3 tablespoons Champagne or sparkling wine (chilled)
- 1 teaspoon vanilla extract
- A pinch of salt

For Garnish (Optional):

- Edible gold or silver glitter
- Fresh berries
- Sugar pearls

Instructions:

1. Prepare the Cupcakes:

1. Preheat your oven to 350°F (175°C). Line a muffin tin with paper liners.
2. In a medium bowl, whisk together the flour, baking powder, and salt.
3. In a large bowl, beat the butter and sugar together until light and fluffy.
4. Add the eggs one at a time, beating well after each addition. Mix in the vanilla extract.
5. Gradually add the flour mixture in three parts, alternating with the Champagne and milk, starting and ending with the flour mixture. Mix until just combined.
6. Divide the batter evenly among the cupcake liners, filling each about 2/3 full.
7. Bake for 18-20 minutes, or until a toothpick inserted into the center comes out clean.
8. Allow the cupcakes to cool in the tin for 5 minutes, then transfer them to a wire rack to cool completely.

2. Make the Champagne Buttercream Frosting:

1. In a large bowl, beat the butter until creamy.
2. Gradually add the powdered sugar, mixing on low speed until combined.
3. Add 2 tablespoons of Champagne, vanilla extract, and a pinch of salt. Beat on high speed until the frosting is light and fluffy. If the frosting is too thick, add more Champagne, 1 teaspoon at a time, until you reach the desired consistency.

3. Frost the Cupcakes:

1. Once the cupcakes are completely cooled, frost them with the Champagne buttercream using a piping bag or a knife.
2. Garnish with edible glitter, fresh berries, or sugar pearls if desired.

Enjoy your celebratory Champagne Cupcakes!

Red Velvet Cheesecake Brownies

Ingredients:

For the Red Velvet Brownies:

- 1/2 cup (115g) unsalted butter
- 1 cup (200g) granulated sugar
- 2 large eggs
- 1 teaspoon vanilla extract
- 1 tablespoon red food coloring (gel or liquid)
- 1 tablespoon cocoa powder
- 1 1/2 cups (190g) all-purpose flour
- 1/4 teaspoon salt
- 1/4 teaspoon baking powder

For the Cheesecake Swirl:

- 8 oz (225g) cream cheese, softened
- 1/4 cup (50g) granulated sugar
- 1 large egg
- 1/2 teaspoon vanilla extract

Instructions:

1. Prepare the Red Velvet Brownie Batter:

1. Preheat your oven to 350°F (175°C). Grease and line an 8x8-inch (20x20 cm) baking pan with parchment paper.
2. In a medium saucepan, melt the butter over low heat. Remove from heat and stir in the sugar, eggs, and vanilla extract.
3. Mix in the red food coloring and cocoa powder until well combined.
4. In a separate bowl, whisk together the flour, salt, and baking powder.
5. Gradually add the dry ingredients to the wet ingredients, mixing until just combined.
6. Pour the brownie batter into the prepared baking pan and spread it evenly.

2. Prepare the Cheesecake Swirl:

1. In a medium bowl, beat the cream cheese until smooth and creamy.
2. Add the sugar, egg, and vanilla extract. Beat until fully combined and smooth.
3. Drop spoonfuls of the cheesecake mixture over the brownie batter. Use a knife or toothpick to swirl the cheesecake mixture into the brownie batter, creating a marbled effect.

3. Bake the Brownies:

1. Bake for 30-35 minutes, or until a toothpick inserted into the center comes out with a few moist crumbs (not wet batter).
2. Allow the brownies to cool completely in the pan on a wire rack before cutting into squares.

Enjoy your Red Velvet Cheesecake Brownies—perfectly rich and indulgent!

Pecan Pie Bars

Ingredients:

For the Crust:

- 1 1/2 cups (190g) all-purpose flour
- 1/4 cup (50g) granulated sugar
- 1/2 teaspoon salt
- 1/2 cup (115g) unsalted butter, cold and cut into small pieces

For the Filling:

- 1 cup (240ml) light corn syrup
- 1 cup (220g) packed brown sugar
- 1/4 cup (60g) unsalted butter, melted
- 3 large eggs
- 1 teaspoon vanilla extract
- 1/4 teaspoon salt
- 1 1/2 cups (150g) pecan halves

Instructions:

1. Prepare the Crust:

1. Preheat your oven to 350°F (175°C). Line a 9x13-inch baking dish with parchment paper, leaving an overhang on the sides for easy removal.
2. In a medium bowl, whisk together the flour, sugar, and salt.
3. Cut in the cold butter using a pastry cutter or your fingers until the mixture resembles coarse crumbs.
4. Press the mixture evenly into the bottom of the prepared baking dish.
5. Bake for 15 minutes, or until the edges are lightly golden.

2. Prepare the Filling:

1. While the crust is baking, in a large bowl, whisk together the corn syrup, brown sugar, melted butter, eggs, vanilla extract, and salt until smooth.
2. Stir in the pecan halves.

3. Assemble and Bake:

1. After the crust has baked for 15 minutes, remove it from the oven.
2. Pour the pecan filling evenly over the partially baked crust.
3. Return to the oven and bake for an additional 25-30 minutes, or until the filling is set and slightly puffed. The center may still be slightly soft but will firm up as it cools.

4. Allow the bars to cool completely in the pan on a wire rack before lifting out and cutting into squares.

Enjoy your Pecan Pie Bars as a delightful and convenient alternative to traditional pecan pie!

Raspberry Almond Linzer Cookies

Ingredients:

For the Cookies:

- 1 3/4 cups (220g) all-purpose flour
- 1/2 teaspoon baking powder
- 1/4 teaspoon salt
- 1/2 cup (115g) unsalted butter, room temperature
- 1/2 cup (100g) granulated sugar
- 1/2 cup (50g) almond meal (finely ground almonds)
- 1 large egg
- 1 teaspoon vanilla extract
- 1/2 teaspoon almond extract

For the Filling:

- 1/2 cup (160g) raspberry jam or preserves (seedless)

For Dusting (Optional):

- Powdered sugar

Instructions:

1. Prepare the Dough:

1. In a medium bowl, whisk together the flour, baking powder, and salt.
2. In a large bowl, beat the butter and granulated sugar until light and fluffy.
3. Mix in the almond meal until well combined.
4. Add the egg, vanilla extract, and almond extract, and beat until smooth.
5. Gradually add the flour mixture, mixing until just combined.
6. Divide the dough in half, shape each half into a disk, and wrap in plastic wrap. Chill in the refrigerator for at least 1 hour, or until firm.

2. Roll and Cut the Cookies:

1. Preheat your oven to 350°F (175°C). Line baking sheets with parchment paper.
2. On a lightly floured surface, roll out one disk of dough to about 1/8-inch thickness.
3. Use a cookie cutter to cut out cookies. For half of the cookies, use a smaller cutter to cut out the center to create a window.
4. Transfer the cookies to the prepared baking sheets.
5. Bake for 8-10 minutes, or until the edges are lightly golden. Let the cookies cool on the baking sheets for a few minutes before transferring to a wire rack to cool completely.

3. Assemble the Cookies:

1. Once the cookies are completely cool, spread a small amount of raspberry jam on the solid cookies.
2. Place the cut-out cookies on top, gently pressing down to sandwich the jam between the layers.
3. (Optional) Dust with powdered sugar before serving.

Enjoy your Raspberry Almond Linzer Cookies! They're perfect for holiday gatherings or as a sweet treat any time of year.

Lemon Blueberry Bundt Cake

Ingredients:

For the Cake:

- 2 1/2 cups (310g) all-purpose flour
- 1 1/2 teaspoons baking powder
- 1/2 teaspoon baking soda
- 1/2 teaspoon salt
- 1/2 cup (115g) unsalted butter, room temperature
- 1 cup (200g) granulated sugar
- 1/2 cup (100g) packed light brown sugar
- 3 large eggs
- 1 cup (240ml) sour cream or Greek yogurt
- 1/2 cup (120ml) whole milk
- 1/4 cup (60ml) fresh lemon juice
- 2 tablespoons lemon zest (from about 2 lemons)
- 1 teaspoon vanilla extract
- 1 1/2 cups (150g) fresh or frozen blueberries (tossed in 1 tablespoon flour)

For the Lemon Glaze:

- 1 cup (120g) powdered sugar
- 2 tablespoons fresh lemon juice
- 1 tablespoon milk (if needed, to adjust consistency)

Instructions:

1. Prepare the Cake:

1. Preheat your oven to 350°F (175°C). Grease and flour a 12-cup Bundt pan, or spray with non-stick baking spray with flour.
2. In a medium bowl, whisk together the flour, baking powder, baking soda, and salt.
3. In a large bowl, beat the butter, granulated sugar, and brown sugar until light and fluffy.
4. Add the eggs one at a time, beating well after each addition.
5. Mix in the sour cream, milk, lemon juice, lemon zest, and vanilla extract until combined.
6. Gradually add the flour mixture, mixing until just combined.
7. Gently fold in the blueberries coated with flour.
8. Pour the batter into the prepared Bundt pan, smoothing the top with a spatula.

2. Bake the Cake:

1. Bake for 50-60 minutes, or until a toothpick inserted into the center comes out clean.
2. Allow the cake to cool in the pan for 15 minutes before transferring it to a wire rack to cool completely.

3. Prepare the Lemon Glaze:

1. In a small bowl, whisk together the powdered sugar and lemon juice until smooth. If the glaze is too thick, add a little milk to reach the desired consistency.

4. Glaze the Cake:

1. Once the cake is completely cool, drizzle the lemon glaze over the top of the cake, allowing it to drip down the sides.

Enjoy your Lemon Blueberry Bundt Cake with a cup of tea or coffee! It's a perfect treat for any occasion.

Eggnog Snickerdoodles

Ingredients:

For the Cookies:

- 2 3/4 cups (340g) all-purpose flour
- 1/2 teaspoon baking soda
- 1/2 teaspoon baking powder
- 1/4 teaspoon salt
- 1/2 teaspoon ground nutmeg
- 1/2 teaspoon ground cinnamon
- 1/2 cup (115g) unsalted butter, room temperature
- 1 cup (200g) granulated sugar
- 1 large egg
- 1/2 cup (120ml) eggnog
- 1 teaspoon vanilla extract

For the Cinnamon-Sugar Coating:

- 1/4 cup (50g) granulated sugar
- 1 teaspoon ground cinnamon
- 1/4 teaspoon ground nutmeg

Instructions:

1. Prepare the Cookie Dough:

1. Preheat your oven to 350°F (175°C). Line baking sheets with parchment paper.
2. In a medium bowl, whisk together the flour, baking soda, baking powder, salt, nutmeg, and cinnamon.
3. In a large bowl, beat the butter and granulated sugar until light and fluffy.
4. Beat in the egg, then mix in the eggnog and vanilla extract until combined.
5. Gradually add the dry ingredients to the wet ingredients, mixing until just combined.

2. Shape and Coat the Cookies:

1. In a small bowl, mix together the granulated sugar, cinnamon, and nutmeg for the coating.
2. Scoop tablespoon-sized balls of dough and roll them into balls. Roll each ball in the cinnamon-sugar mixture until fully coated.
3. Place the coated dough balls on the prepared baking sheets, spacing them about 2 inches apart.

3. Bake the Cookies:

1. Bake for 10-12 minutes, or until the edges are set and the tops have slightly cracked.
2. Let the cookies cool on the baking sheets for a few minutes before transferring them to a wire rack to cool completely.

Enjoy your Eggnog Snickerdoodles with a glass of eggnog or as a sweet holiday treat!

Salted Caramel Brownies

Ingredients:

For the Brownies:

- 1/2 cup (115g) unsalted butter
- 1 cup (200g) granulated sugar
- 1/4 cup (50g) packed light brown sugar
- 2 large eggs
- 1 teaspoon vanilla extract
- 1/3 cup (30g) unsweetened cocoa powder
- 1/2 cup (65g) all-purpose flour
- 1/4 teaspoon salt
- 1/4 teaspoon baking powder

For the Salted Caramel Layer:

- 1 cup (200g) granulated sugar
- 6 tablespoons (85g) unsalted butter, cut into pieces
- 1/2 cup (120ml) heavy cream
- 1/2 teaspoon sea salt (or to taste)

Instructions:

1. Prepare the Caramel Layer:

1. In a medium saucepan over medium heat, melt the granulated sugar, stirring constantly until it turns into a deep amber color.
2. Carefully add the butter to the melted sugar, stirring continuously. The mixture will bubble up.
3. Once the butter is fully incorporated, slowly pour in the heavy cream while continuing to stir. Be careful, as the mixture will bubble vigorously.
4. Cook for another 2-3 minutes, stirring constantly, until the caramel is smooth and thickened.
5. Remove from heat and stir in the sea salt. Let the caramel cool slightly while you prepare the brownie batter.

2. Prepare the Brownies:

1. Preheat your oven to 350°F (175°C). Grease and line an 8x8-inch (20x20 cm) baking pan with parchment paper, leaving an overhang for easy removal.
2. In a medium saucepan, melt the butter over low heat. Remove from heat and stir in the granulated sugar and brown sugar until well combined.
3. Beat in the eggs, one at a time, followed by the vanilla extract.
4. Mix in the cocoa powder until smooth.

5. Add the flour, salt, and baking powder, and stir until just combined.
6. Pour the brownie batter into the prepared pan, spreading it evenly.

3. Add the Caramel Layer:

1. Drop spoonfuls of the caramel sauce over the brownie batter. Use a knife or toothpick to swirl the caramel into the batter, creating a marbled effect.

4. Bake the Brownies:

1. Bake for 25-30 minutes, or until a toothpick inserted into the center comes out with a few moist crumbs (not wet batter).
2. Allow the brownies to cool in the pan on a wire rack before cutting into squares.

Enjoy your indulgent Salted Caramel Brownies—rich, gooey, and perfect for any occasion!

Sparkling Lemon Bars

Ingredients:

For the Crust:

- 1 1/2 cups (190g) all-purpose flour
- 1/4 cup (50g) granulated sugar
- 1/4 teaspoon salt
- 1/2 cup (115g) unsalted butter, cold and cut into small pieces

For the Lemon Filling:

- 1 cup (200g) granulated sugar
- 2 tablespoons all-purpose flour
- 1/4 teaspoon salt
- 3 large eggs
- 1/2 cup (120ml) freshly squeezed lemon juice (about 2-3 lemons)
- 2 tablespoons lemon zest (from about 2 lemons)

For the Sparkling Topping:

- 2 tablespoons granulated sugar
- 1/2 teaspoon lemon zest

Instructions:

1. Prepare the Crust:

1. Preheat your oven to 350°F (175°C). Grease and line an 8x8-inch (20x20 cm) baking pan with parchment paper, leaving an overhang for easy removal.
2. In a medium bowl, whisk together the flour, sugar, and salt.
3. Cut in the cold butter using a pastry cutter or your fingers until the mixture resembles coarse crumbs.
4. Press the mixture evenly into the bottom of the prepared baking pan.
5. Bake for 15 minutes, or until the edges are lightly golden.

2. Prepare the Lemon Filling:

1. In a medium bowl, whisk together the sugar, flour, and salt.
2. Add the eggs and whisk until fully combined.
3. Stir in the lemon juice and lemon zest until smooth.
4. Pour the lemon filling over the partially baked crust.

3. Bake and Add the Topping:

1. Bake for an additional 20-25 minutes, or until the lemon filling is set and slightly firm to the touch.
2. While the lemon bars are baking, prepare the sparkling topping by mixing the granulated sugar and lemon zest in a small bowl.
3. Immediately after removing the bars from the oven, sprinkle the sparkling sugar mixture evenly over the top.

4. Cool and Serve:

1. Allow the lemon bars to cool completely in the pan on a wire rack.
2. Once cooled, lift the bars out of the pan using the parchment paper overhang and cut into squares.

Enjoy your Sparkling Lemon Bars—tangy, sweet, and with a delightful touch of sparkle!

Mocha Hazelnut Tart

Ingredients:

For the Hazelnut Crust:

- 1 cup (120g) hazelnuts (toasted and skins removed)
- 1/2 cup (65g) all-purpose flour
- 1/4 cup (50g) granulated sugar
- 1/4 teaspoon salt
- 1/4 cup (55g) unsalted butter, cold and cut into small pieces
- 1 large egg yolk

For the Mocha Filling:

- 1/2 cup (120ml) heavy cream
- 1/2 cup (120ml) brewed strong coffee or espresso (cooled)
- 8 oz (225g) semi-sweet or bittersweet chocolate, chopped
- 2 large eggs
- 1/4 cup (50g) granulated sugar
- 1 teaspoon vanilla extract
- 1 tablespoon unsweetened cocoa powder
- 1/4 teaspoon salt

For the Garnish (Optional):

- Whipped cream
- Shaved chocolate
- Chopped hazelnuts

Instructions:

1. Prepare the Hazelnut Crust:

1. Preheat your oven to 350°F (175°C). Lightly grease a 9-inch (23 cm) tart pan with a removable bottom.
2. In a food processor, pulse the toasted hazelnuts until finely ground.
3. Add the flour, sugar, and salt, and pulse to combine.
4. Add the cold butter and pulse until the mixture resembles coarse crumbs.
5. Add the egg yolk and pulse until the dough starts to come together.
6. Press the dough evenly into the bottom and up the sides of the prepared tart pan.
7. Bake for 15 minutes, or until the crust is lightly golden. Let it cool completely on a wire rack.

2. Prepare the Mocha Filling:

1. In a small saucepan, heat the heavy cream until it just begins to simmer. Remove from heat.
2. Add the chopped chocolate to the hot cream and let it sit for a few minutes until melted. Stir until smooth.
3. Stir in the brewed coffee or espresso until fully combined.
4. In a medium bowl, whisk together the eggs, sugar, vanilla extract, cocoa powder, and salt.
5. Gradually add the chocolate mixture to the egg mixture, whisking continuously until smooth and combined.

3. Assemble and Bake the Tart:

1. Pour the mocha filling into the cooled hazelnut crust.
2. Bake for 20-25 minutes, or until the filling is set and the center is slightly jiggly.
3. Allow the tart to cool completely in the pan on a wire rack. The filling will firm up as it cools.

4. Garnish and Serve:

1. Once the tart is completely cooled, garnish with whipped cream, shaved chocolate, and chopped hazelnuts if desired.
2. Slice and serve.

Enjoy your Mocha Hazelnut Tart—a rich, chocolatey treat with a delightful hint of coffee and a crunchy hazelnut crust!

Apple Cider Donuts

Ingredients:

For the Donuts:

- 1 cup (240ml) apple cider
- 1/2 cup (115g) unsalted butter
- 1 large egg
- 1 cup (200g) granulated sugar
- 2 teaspoons ground cinnamon
- 1/2 teaspoon ground nutmeg
- 1/2 teaspoon ground allspice
- 1/4 teaspoon ground cloves
- 2 1/4 cups (280g) all-purpose flour
- 2 teaspoons baking powder
- 1/2 teaspoon baking soda
- 1/2 teaspoon salt

For the Cinnamon Sugar Coating:

- 1/2 cup (100g) granulated sugar
- 2 teaspoons ground cinnamon

Instructions:

1. Reduce the Apple Cider:

1. In a small saucepan over medium heat, bring the apple cider to a boil.
2. Reduce the heat and simmer until the cider is reduced to about 1/2 cup (120ml) and slightly thickened. This should take about 10-15 minutes.
3. Remove from heat and let it cool to room temperature.

2. Prepare the Donut Batter:

1. Preheat your oven to 350°F (175°C). Grease a donut pan or lightly spray it with non-stick cooking spray.
2. In a medium bowl, whisk together the flour, baking powder, baking soda, salt, cinnamon, nutmeg, allspice, and cloves.
3. In a large bowl, beat the butter and sugar until light and fluffy.
4. Add the egg and beat until combined.
5. Mix in the cooled reduced apple cider.
6. Gradually add the dry ingredients, mixing until just combined.

3. Fill and Bake:

1. Spoon the batter into the prepared donut pan, filling each cavity about 2/3 full.
2. Bake for 12-15 minutes, or until a toothpick inserted into the center comes out clean.
3. Allow the donuts to cool in the pan for a few minutes before transferring them to a wire rack to cool completely.

4. Coat the Donuts:

1. In a small bowl, mix the granulated sugar and cinnamon for the coating.
2. Once the donuts are completely cool, lightly brush or dip them in melted butter.
3. Roll the donuts in the cinnamon sugar mixture until well coated.

Enjoy your homemade Apple Cider Donuts—perfect with a cup of coffee or cider for a cozy treat!

Cream Cheese Sugar Cookies

Ingredients:

For the Cookies:

- 1/2 cup (115g) unsalted butter, room temperature
- 1/2 cup (115g) cream cheese, softened
- 1 cup (200g) granulated sugar
- 1 large egg
- 1 teaspoon vanilla extract
- 2 1/4 cups (280g) all-purpose flour
- 1/2 teaspoon baking powder
- 1/4 teaspoon salt

For the Sugar Coating (Optional):

- 1/4 cup (50g) granulated sugar
- 1 teaspoon ground cinnamon

Instructions:

1. Prepare the Cookie Dough:

1. In a large bowl, beat the butter and cream cheese together until smooth and creamy.
2. Add the granulated sugar and beat until light and fluffy.
3. Beat in the egg and vanilla extract until well combined.
4. In a separate bowl, whisk together the flour, baking powder, and salt.
5. Gradually add the dry ingredients to the wet ingredients, mixing until just combined.

2. Chill the Dough:

1. Divide the dough into two portions and wrap each portion in plastic wrap.
2. Chill in the refrigerator for at least 1 hour, or until firm. Chilling helps the cookies maintain their shape during baking.

3. Shape and Bake:

1. Preheat your oven to 350°F (175°C). Line baking sheets with parchment paper or silicone baking mats.
2. On a lightly floured surface, roll out one portion of the dough to about 1/4-inch thickness.
3. Use cookie cutters to cut out shapes and transfer them to the prepared baking sheets. Alternatively, you can roll the dough into balls and flatten them slightly with the bottom of a glass.
4. If using, mix the granulated sugar and cinnamon for the coating. Sprinkle or dip the cookies in the mixture before baking.

5. Bake for 10-12 minutes, or until the edges are lightly golden.
6. Allow the cookies to cool on the baking sheets for a few minutes before transferring them to a wire rack to cool completely.

4. Decorate (Optional):

- If desired, you can decorate the cooled cookies with icing or sprinkles.

Enjoy your Cream Cheese Sugar Cookies—they're soft, slightly tangy, and perfect for any occasion!

Black Forest Cake

Ingredients:

For the Chocolate Cake:

- 1 3/4 cups (220g) all-purpose flour
- 2 cups (400g) granulated sugar
- 3/4 cup (65g) unsweetened cocoa powder
- 1 1/2 teaspoons baking powder
- 1 1/2 teaspoons baking soda
- 1/2 teaspoon salt
- 2 large eggs
- 1 cup (240ml) whole milk
- 1/2 cup (120ml) vegetable oil
- 2 teaspoons vanilla extract
- 1 cup (240ml) boiling water

For the Cherry Filling:

- 1 jar (about 24 oz or 680g) Morello cherries, drained and pitted (reserve some juice)
- 1/4 cup (50g) granulated sugar
- 1 tablespoon cornstarch
- 1 tablespoon lemon juice

For the Whipped Cream:

- 2 cups (480ml) heavy cream
- 1/2 cup (60g) powdered sugar
- 1 teaspoon vanilla extract

For Assembly and Decoration:

- 1/2 cup (120ml) kirsch (cherry brandy) or cherry juice (for soaking)
- Chocolate shavings or curls
- Additional cherries for decoration

Instructions:

1. Prepare the Chocolate Cake:

1. Preheat your oven to 350°F (175°C). Grease and flour two 9-inch (23 cm) round cake pans.
2. In a large bowl, sift together the flour, sugar, cocoa powder, baking powder, baking soda, and salt.

3. Add the eggs, milk, vegetable oil, and vanilla extract. Beat on medium speed until smooth.
4. Stir in the boiling water until the batter is well combined (it will be thin).
5. Divide the batter evenly between the prepared pans.
6. Bake for 30-35 minutes, or until a toothpick inserted into the center comes out clean.
7. Allow the cakes to cool in the pans for 10 minutes before transferring them to a wire rack to cool completely.

2. Prepare the Cherry Filling:

1. In a medium saucepan, combine the cherries, sugar, cornstarch, and lemon juice.
2. Cook over medium heat, stirring constantly, until the mixture thickens and becomes clear. This should take about 5-7 minutes.
3. Remove from heat and let it cool completely.

3. Prepare the Whipped Cream:

1. In a large bowl, beat the heavy cream, powdered sugar, and vanilla extract until stiff peaks form.

4. Assemble the Cake:

1. Once the cakes are completely cooled, level the tops if necessary.
2. Place one cake layer on a serving plate or cake stand. Brush with half of the kirsch (or cherry juice) to soak.
3. Spread a layer of whipped cream over the cake layer, followed by a portion of the cherry filling.
4. Place the second cake layer on top. Brush with the remaining kirsch.
5. Frost the top and sides of the cake with the remaining whipped cream.

5. Decorate the Cake:

1. Garnish with chocolate shavings or curls and additional cherries.

Enjoy your Black Forest Cake—rich, creamy, and a classic favorite!

Maple Walnut Scones

Ingredients:

For the Scones:

- 2 cups (250g) all-purpose flour
- 1/4 cup (50g) granulated sugar
- 1 tablespoon baking powder
- 1/2 teaspoon salt
- 1/2 cup (115g) unsalted butter, cold and cut into small pieces
- 1/2 cup (120ml) pure maple syrup
- 1/4 cup (60ml) heavy cream
- 1 large egg
- 1/2 cup (60g) chopped walnuts

For the Maple Glaze (Optional):

- 1/2 cup (60g) powdered sugar
- 2 tablespoons pure maple syrup
- 1-2 tablespoons milk (to adjust consistency)

Instructions:

1. Prepare the Scone Dough:

1. Preheat your oven to 400°F (200°C). Line a baking sheet with parchment paper.
2. In a large bowl, whisk together the flour, granulated sugar, baking powder, and salt.
3. Cut in the cold butter using a pastry cutter or your fingers until the mixture resembles coarse crumbs.
4. In a separate bowl, whisk together the maple syrup, heavy cream, and egg.
5. Pour the wet ingredients into the dry ingredients and stir until just combined. The dough will be sticky.
6. Gently fold in the chopped walnuts.

2. Shape and Bake the Scones:

1. Turn the dough out onto a lightly floured surface and gently knead it a few times to bring it together.
2. Pat the dough into a 1-inch thick circle. Cut the dough into 8 wedges (or use a round cutter for circular scones).
3. Place the scone wedges onto the prepared baking sheet, spacing them about 2 inches apart.
4. Bake for 15-18 minutes, or until the scones are golden brown and cooked through.

3. Prepare the Maple Glaze (Optional):

1. In a small bowl, whisk together the powdered sugar and maple syrup until smooth.
2. If needed, add milk a little at a time until the glaze reaches the desired consistency.

4. Glaze and Serve:

1. Allow the scones to cool slightly on a wire rack before drizzling with the maple glaze.
2. Serve warm or at room temperature.

Enjoy your Maple Walnut Scones with a cup of coffee or tea! They're a perfect treat for any time of day.

Mint Chocolate Chip Muffins

Ingredients:

For the Muffins:

- 1 3/4 cups (220g) all-purpose flour
- 1/2 cup (100g) granulated sugar
- 1/4 cup (50g) packed light brown sugar
- 2 teaspoons baking powder
- 1/2 teaspoon baking soda
- 1/4 teaspoon salt
- 1/2 cup (115g) unsalted butter, melted
- 1 large egg
- 1 cup (240ml) buttermilk (or milk with 1 tablespoon lemon juice or vinegar)
- 1 teaspoon peppermint extract
- 1/2 cup (90g) mini chocolate chips
- 1/2 cup (60g) chopped mint chocolate (optional for extra minty flavor)

For the Sugar Topping (Optional):

- 2 tablespoons granulated sugar
- 1/2 teaspoon crushed peppermint candies or candy canes (for a festive touch)

Instructions:

1. Prepare the Muffin Batter:

1. Preheat your oven to 375°F (190°C). Line a muffin tin with paper liners or lightly grease the cups.
2. In a large bowl, whisk together the flour, granulated sugar, brown sugar, baking powder, baking soda, and salt.
3. In another bowl, whisk together the melted butter, egg, buttermilk, and peppermint extract until well combined.
4. Add the wet ingredients to the dry ingredients and stir until just combined. The batter will be lumpy.
5. Gently fold in the mini chocolate chips and chopped mint chocolate (if using).

2. Fill the Muffin Tin:

1. Divide the muffin batter evenly among the muffin cups, filling each about 3/4 full.

3. Add the Sugar Topping (Optional):

1. In a small bowl, mix the granulated sugar with crushed peppermint candies or candy canes.

2. Sprinkle the mixture over the top of each muffin before baking.

4. Bake the Muffins:

1. Bake for 18-22 minutes, or until a toothpick inserted into the center of a muffin comes out clean.
2. Allow the muffins to cool in the pan for about 5 minutes before transferring them to a wire rack to cool completely.

Enjoy your Mint Chocolate Chip Muffins with a cup of tea or coffee, or simply on their own for a minty, chocolatey treat!

White Chocolate Cranberry Blondies

Ingredients:

For the Blondies:

- 1/2 cup (115g) unsalted butter, melted
- 1 cup (200g) packed brown sugar
- 1/4 cup (50g) granulated sugar
- 1 large egg
- 1 teaspoon vanilla extract
- 1 1/2 cups (190g) all-purpose flour
- 1/2 teaspoon baking powder
- 1/4 teaspoon salt
- 1 cup (175g) white chocolate chips or chunks
- 1 cup (120g) dried cranberries

For the Optional Drizzle:

- 1/2 cup (90g) white chocolate chips
- 1 tablespoon heavy cream

Instructions:

1. Prepare the Blondie Batter:

1. Preheat your oven to 350°F (175°C). Grease and line an 8x8-inch (20x20 cm) baking pan with parchment paper, leaving an overhang for easy removal.
2. In a large bowl, mix the melted butter with the brown sugar and granulated sugar until well combined and smooth.
3. Beat in the egg and vanilla extract.
4. In a separate bowl, whisk together the flour, baking powder, and salt.
5. Gradually add the dry ingredients to the wet ingredients, mixing until just combined.
6. Fold in the white chocolate chips and dried cranberries.

2. Bake the Blondies:

1. Pour the batter into the prepared baking pan and spread it evenly.
2. Bake for 25-30 minutes, or until a toothpick inserted into the center comes out with a few moist crumbs (not wet batter).
3. Allow the blondies to cool completely in the pan on a wire rack before lifting them out using the parchment paper and cutting into squares.

3. Prepare the Optional Drizzle:

1. In a small heatproof bowl, combine the white chocolate chips and heavy cream.

2. Melt in the microwave in 20-second intervals, stirring in between, until smooth and fully melted.
3. Drizzle the melted white chocolate over the cooled blondies.

4. Serve:

1. Cut the blondies into squares and enjoy!

These White Chocolate Cranberry Blondies are sweet, chewy, and packed with delicious flavors—perfect for any dessert table or a special treat!

Pumpkin Spice Bundt Cake

Ingredients:

For the Cake:

- 1 1/2 cups (190g) all-purpose flour
- 1 teaspoon baking powder
- 1/2 teaspoon baking soda
- 1/2 teaspoon salt
- 1 teaspoon ground cinnamon
- 1/2 teaspoon ground ginger
- 1/4 teaspoon ground nutmeg
- 1/4 teaspoon ground cloves
- 1/2 cup (115g) unsalted butter, softened
- 1 cup (200g) granulated sugar
- 1/2 cup (100g) packed light brown sugar
- 2 large eggs
- 1 cup (240ml) canned pumpkin puree (not pumpkin pie filling)
- 1/2 cup (120ml) buttermilk (or milk with 1 tablespoon lemon juice or vinegar)
- 1 teaspoon vanilla extract

For the Glaze (Optional):

- 1 cup (120g) powdered sugar
- 2-3 tablespoons milk
- 1/2 teaspoon vanilla extract
- 1/4 teaspoon ground cinnamon

Instructions:

1. Prepare the Cake Batter:

1. Preheat your oven to 350°F (175°C). Grease and flour a 10-inch Bundt pan, or use a non-stick Bundt pan.
2. In a medium bowl, whisk together the flour, baking powder, baking soda, salt, cinnamon, ginger, nutmeg, and cloves.
3. In a large bowl, beat the softened butter, granulated sugar, and brown sugar until light and fluffy.
4. Beat in the eggs, one at a time, until well combined.
5. Mix in the pumpkin puree until smooth.
6. Gradually add the dry ingredients to the wet ingredients, alternating with the buttermilk, beginning and ending with the dry ingredients. Mix until just combined.
7. Stir in the vanilla extract.

2. Bake the Cake:

1. Pour the batter into the prepared Bundt pan and smooth the top with a spatula.
2. Bake for 45-55 minutes, or until a toothpick inserted into the center comes out clean.
3. Allow the cake to cool in the pan for about 15 minutes before inverting it onto a wire rack to cool completely.

3. Prepare the Glaze (Optional):

1. In a small bowl, whisk together the powdered sugar, milk, vanilla extract, and ground cinnamon until smooth. Add more milk if needed to reach the desired consistency.

4. Glaze and Serve:

1. Once the cake has completely cooled, drizzle the glaze over the top.
2. Let the glaze set before slicing and serving.

Enjoy your Pumpkin Spice Bundt Cake with a cup of coffee or tea, or simply on its own as a delightful fall treat!

Almond Joy Cheesecake

Ingredients:

For the Crust:

- 1 1/2 cups (150g) graham cracker crumbs
- 1/4 cup (50g) granulated sugar
- 1/2 cup (115g) unsalted butter, melted

For the Cheesecake Filling:

- 4 (8 oz each) (900g) packages cream cheese, softened
- 1 cup (200g) granulated sugar
- 1 teaspoon vanilla extract
- 4 large eggs
- 1 cup (240ml) sour cream
- 1 cup (240ml) heavy cream
- 1 cup (100g) shredded sweetened coconut
- 1/2 cup (80g) chopped almonds

For the Topping:

- 1 cup (240ml) heavy cream
- 1/4 cup (30g) powdered sugar
- 1/2 teaspoon vanilla extract
- 1/2 cup (80g) chopped almonds
- 1/2 cup (90g) chocolate chips (or chopped chocolate)
- 2 tablespoons coconut oil or vegetable oil

Instructions:

1. Prepare the Crust:

1. Preheat your oven to 325°F (165°C). Lightly grease a 9-inch (23 cm) springform pan.
2. In a medium bowl, combine the graham cracker crumbs, granulated sugar, and melted butter. Mix until the crumbs are evenly coated.
3. Press the mixture firmly into the bottom of the prepared springform pan.
4. Bake for 8-10 minutes, then remove from the oven and let it cool while you prepare the filling.

2. Prepare the Cheesecake Filling:

1. In a large mixing bowl, beat the cream cheese until smooth and creamy.
2. Add the granulated sugar and vanilla extract, and beat until well combined.
3. Beat in the eggs, one at a time, mixing well after each addition.

4. Add the sour cream and heavy cream, and mix until smooth.
5. Gently fold in the shredded coconut and chopped almonds.
6. Pour the filling over the cooled crust in the springform pan.

3. Bake the Cheesecake:

1. Bake the cheesecake for 55-65 minutes, or until the center is set but still slightly jiggly.
2. Turn off the oven, crack the oven door slightly, and let the cheesecake cool in the oven for 1 hour.
3. Remove the cheesecake from the oven and refrigerate for at least 4 hours or overnight.

4. Prepare the Topping:

1. In a medium bowl, whip the heavy cream, powdered sugar, and vanilla extract until stiff peaks form.
2. Spread or pipe the whipped cream over the chilled cheesecake.
3. In a small microwave-safe bowl, melt the chocolate chips with coconut oil or vegetable oil in 20-second intervals, stirring in between until smooth.
4. Drizzle the melted chocolate over the whipped cream.
5. Sprinkle the chopped almonds on top.

5. Serve:

1. Release the sides of the springform pan and transfer the cheesecake to a serving plate.
2. Slice and enjoy your Almond Joy Cheesecake!

This rich and creamy cheesecake brings together the flavors of chocolate, almond, and coconut in a decadent dessert that's perfect for any special occasion.

Tiramisu Cupcakes

Ingredients:

For the Cupcakes:

- 1 1/2 cups (190g) all-purpose flour
- 1 1/2 teaspoons baking powder
- 1/4 teaspoon salt
- 1/2 cup (115g) unsalted butter, room temperature
- 1 cup (200g) granulated sugar
- 2 large eggs
- 1/2 cup (120ml) whole milk
- 1/2 cup (120ml) strong brewed coffee, cooled
- 1 teaspoon vanilla extract

For the Coffee Soak:

- 1/4 cup (60ml) strong brewed coffee
- 2 tablespoons coffee liqueur (e.g., Kahlúa) or additional brewed coffee (optional)

For the Mascarpone Frosting:

- 8 oz (225g) mascarpone cheese, softened
- 1 cup (240ml) heavy cream
- 1/2 cup (60g) powdered sugar
- 1 teaspoon vanilla extract
- Unsweetened cocoa powder (for dusting)

Instructions:

1. Prepare the Cupcakes:

1. Preheat your oven to 350°F (175°C). Line a 12-cup muffin tin with paper liners.
2. In a medium bowl, whisk together the flour, baking powder, and salt.
3. In a large bowl, beat the butter and granulated sugar until light and fluffy.
4. Beat in the eggs, one at a time, until well combined.
5. Mix in the milk, brewed coffee, and vanilla extract.
6. Gradually add the dry ingredients to the wet ingredients, mixing until just combined.
7. Divide the batter evenly among the cupcake liners, filling each about 2/3 full.
8. Bake for 18-20 minutes, or until a toothpick inserted into the center of a cupcake comes out clean.
9. Allow the cupcakes to cool in the tin for 5 minutes, then transfer to a wire rack to cool completely.

2. Prepare the Coffee Soak:

1. In a small bowl, combine the brewed coffee with coffee liqueur (if using). Stir well.

3. Soak the Cupcakes:

1. Once the cupcakes have cooled, use a toothpick or skewer to poke small holes in the tops of each cupcake.
2. Brush or drizzle the coffee soak evenly over the tops of the cupcakes, allowing it to soak in.

4. Prepare the Mascarpone Frosting:

1. In a large bowl, beat the mascarpone cheese until smooth.
2. In another bowl, whip the heavy cream, powdered sugar, and vanilla extract until stiff peaks form.
3. Gently fold the whipped cream into the mascarpone cheese until fully combined and smooth.

5. Frost and Decorate:

1. Frost the cooled cupcakes with the mascarpone frosting using a piping bag or a spatula.
2. Dust the tops with unsweetened cocoa powder for a finishing touch.

Enjoy your Tiramisu Cupcakes—an elegant and delightful twist on the classic Italian dessert!

Chocolate Chip Pumpkin Bread

Ingredients:

For the Bread:

- 1 3/4 cups (220g) all-purpose flour
- 1 teaspoon baking powder
- 1/2 teaspoon baking soda
- 1/2 teaspoon salt
- 1 teaspoon ground cinnamon
- 1/2 teaspoon ground nutmeg
- 1/4 teaspoon ground cloves
- 1/4 teaspoon ground ginger
- 1/2 cup (115g) unsalted butter, room temperature
- 1 cup (200g) granulated sugar
- 1/2 cup (100g) packed light brown sugar
- 2 large eggs
- 1 cup (240ml) canned pumpkin puree (not pumpkin pie filling)
- 1/4 cup (60ml) milk (whole or 2%)
- 1 teaspoon vanilla extract
- 1 cup (175g) semi-sweet chocolate chips

For the Optional Glaze:

- 1/2 cup (60g) powdered sugar
- 1-2 tablespoons milk
- 1/4 teaspoon vanilla extract

Instructions:

1. Prepare the Bread Batter:

1. Preheat your oven to 350°F (175°C). Grease and flour a 9x5-inch (23x13 cm) loaf pan.
2. In a medium bowl, whisk together the flour, baking powder, baking soda, salt, cinnamon, nutmeg, cloves, and ginger.
3. In a large bowl, beat the butter, granulated sugar, and brown sugar until light and fluffy.
4. Add the eggs, one at a time, beating well after each addition.
5. Mix in the pumpkin puree, milk, and vanilla extract.
6. Gradually add the dry ingredients to the wet ingredients, mixing until just combined.
7. Fold in the chocolate chips.

2. Bake the Bread:

1. Pour the batter into the prepared loaf pan and smooth the top with a spatula.

2. Bake for 60-70 minutes, or until a toothpick inserted into the center comes out clean or with a few moist crumbs.
3. Allow the bread to cool in the pan for 10 minutes before transferring it to a wire rack to cool completely.

3. Prepare the Optional Glaze (if using):

1. In a small bowl, whisk together the powdered sugar, milk, and vanilla extract until smooth. Add more milk if needed to reach the desired consistency.
2. Drizzle the glaze over the cooled bread.

Enjoy your Chocolate Chip Pumpkin Bread—perfectly spiced, wonderfully moist, and studded with chocolate chips!

Vanilla Bean Panna Cotta

Ingredients:

For the Panna Cotta:

- 1 cup (240ml) whole milk
- 1 cup (240ml) heavy cream
- 1/2 cup (100g) granulated sugar
- 1 vanilla bean (or 2 teaspoons pure vanilla extract)
- 1 packet (1/4 oz or 7g) unflavored gelatin powder
- 2 tablespoons (30ml) cold water

For the Optional Berry Sauce:

- 1 cup (150g) mixed berries (fresh or frozen)
- 1/4 cup (50g) granulated sugar
- 1 tablespoon lemon juice

Instructions:

1. Prepare the Panna Cotta:

1. In a small bowl, sprinkle the gelatin powder over the cold water and let it sit for 5-10 minutes to bloom.
2. Split the vanilla bean lengthwise and scrape the seeds out with the back of a knife. If using vanilla extract, you'll add it later.
3. In a medium saucepan, combine the milk, heavy cream, and granulated sugar. Add the vanilla bean seeds and the scraped vanilla pod to the saucepan (or add the vanilla extract later).
4. Heat the mixture over medium heat, stirring frequently, until the sugar is dissolved and the mixture is hot but not boiling. Remove from heat.
5. Add the bloomed gelatin to the hot cream mixture and stir until completely dissolved. Remove and discard the vanilla bean pod if used.
6. If using vanilla extract, stir it in now.
7. Pour the mixture into individual serving glasses or ramekins.

2. Chill the Panna Cotta:

1. Allow the panna cotta to cool slightly before transferring it to the refrigerator.
2. Chill for at least 4 hours, or until set.

3. Prepare the Optional Berry Sauce (if using):

1. In a small saucepan, combine the berries, granulated sugar, and lemon juice.

2. Cook over medium heat, stirring occasionally, until the berries break down and the sauce thickens, about 5-7 minutes.
3. Remove from heat and let it cool to room temperature. The sauce will thicken further as it cools.

4. Serve:

1. Once the panna cotta has set, spoon the berry sauce over the top (if using) just before serving.
2. Garnish with fresh mint leaves or additional berries if desired.

Enjoy your Vanilla Bean Panna Cotta—creamy, smooth, and subtly sweet, with a touch of sophistication!

Carrot Cake Whoopie Pies

Ingredients:

For the Carrot Cake Cookies:

- 2 cups (250g) all-purpose flour
- 1 teaspoon baking powder
- 1/2 teaspoon baking soda
- 1/2 teaspoon salt
- 1 teaspoon ground cinnamon
- 1/2 teaspoon ground ginger
- 1/4 teaspoon ground nutmeg
- 1/4 teaspoon ground cloves
- 1/2 cup (115g) unsalted butter, softened
- 1 cup (200g) granulated sugar
- 1/2 cup (100g) packed light brown sugar
- 2 large eggs
- 1 cup (240ml) grated carrots (about 2 medium carrots)
- 1/2 cup (80g) crushed pineapple, drained
- 1/2 cup (50g) chopped walnuts or pecans (optional)
- 1/2 cup (80g) raisins or currants (optional)

For the Cream Cheese Filling:

- 8 oz (225g) cream cheese, softened
- 1/2 cup (115g) unsalted butter, softened
- 2 cups (240g) powdered sugar
- 1 teaspoon vanilla extract

Instructions:

1. Prepare the Carrot Cake Cookies:

1. Preheat your oven to 350°F (175°C). Line a baking sheet with parchment paper or a silicone baking mat.
2. In a medium bowl, whisk together the flour, baking powder, baking soda, salt, cinnamon, ginger, nutmeg, and cloves.
3. In a large bowl, beat the butter, granulated sugar, and brown sugar until light and fluffy.
4. Beat in the eggs, one at a time, until well combined.
5. Mix in the grated carrots and crushed pineapple.
6. Gradually add the dry ingredients to the wet ingredients, mixing until just combined.
7. Fold in the chopped nuts and raisins or currants, if using.
8. Using a tablespoon or a cookie scoop, drop rounded mounds of dough onto the prepared baking sheet, spacing them about 2 inches apart.
9. Bake for 12-15 minutes, or until the edges are lightly golden and the centers are set.

10. Allow the cookies to cool on the baking sheet for 5 minutes before transferring them to a wire rack to cool completely.

2. Prepare the Cream Cheese Filling:

1. In a medium bowl, beat the cream cheese and butter until smooth and creamy.
2. Gradually add the powdered sugar, beating until well combined and fluffy.
3. Mix in the vanilla extract.

3. Assemble the Whoopie Pies:

1. Once the cookies have cooled, spread a generous amount of cream cheese filling on the flat side of one cookie.
2. Top with another cookie, pressing gently to sandwich the filling.
3. Repeat with the remaining cookies and filling.

4. Serve and Enjoy:

1. Enjoy the whoopie pies immediately or store them in an airtight container in the refrigerator for up to 5 days.

These Carrot Cake Whoopie Pies offer a wonderful combination of moist carrot cake and creamy frosting, perfect for any sweet tooth!

Strawberry Shortcake Bars

Ingredients:

For the Crust:

- 1 ½ cups all-purpose flour
- ½ cup granulated sugar
- ½ cup cold unsalted butter, cut into small pieces
- ¼ teaspoon salt

For the Filling:

- 2 cups fresh strawberries, hulled and sliced
- ¼ cup granulated sugar
- 1 tablespoon cornstarch
- 1 tablespoon lemon juice

For the Topping:

- 1 cup all-purpose flour
- ½ cup granulated sugar
- ½ teaspoon baking powder
- ¼ teaspoon salt
- ¼ cup cold unsalted butter, cut into small pieces
- ¼ cup milk
- ½ teaspoon vanilla extract

Instructions:

1. **Preheat Oven:** Preheat your oven to 350°F (175°C). Grease a 9x9-inch baking pan or line it with parchment paper.
2. **Prepare the Crust:**
    - In a medium bowl, combine the flour, sugar, and salt.
    - Cut in the cold butter using a pastry cutter or your fingers until the mixture resembles coarse crumbs.
    - Press the mixture evenly into the bottom of the prepared pan.
    - Bake for 12-15 minutes, or until lightly golden. Remove from the oven and let cool slightly.
3. **Prepare the Strawberry Filling:**
    - In a medium saucepan, combine the strawberries, sugar, cornstarch, and lemon juice.
    - Cook over medium heat, stirring constantly until the mixture thickens and becomes bubbly, about 5-7 minutes.
    - Remove from heat and let cool slightly.
4. **Prepare the Topping:**

        - In a medium bowl, mix together the flour, sugar, baking powder, and salt.
        - Cut in the cold butter until the mixture resembles coarse crumbs.
        - Stir in the milk and vanilla extract until just combined. The mixture will be a bit lumpy.
5. **Assemble the Bars:**
        - Spread the strawberry filling evenly over the pre-baked crust.
        - Drop spoonfuls of the topping over the strawberry filling. It doesn't have to be perfectly spread out; some of the filling will peek through.
6. **Bake:**
        - Bake for 25-30 minutes, or until the topping is golden brown and the filling is bubbly.
        - Let the bars cool completely in the pan on a wire rack before cutting into squares.
7. **Serve:**
        - Serve chilled or at room temperature. Enjoy with a dollop of whipped cream or a scoop of vanilla ice cream if desired!

These bars combine the classic flavors of strawberry shortcake in a convenient, portable form. Enjoy baking and indulging in these sweet treats!

Espresso Macarons

Ingredients:

For the Macaron Shells:

- 1 cup (100g) almond flour
- 1 ½ cups (150g) powdered sugar
- 3 large egg whites (aged at room temperature)
- ¼ cup (50g) granulated sugar
- 2 tablespoons finely ground espresso beans or instant espresso powder
- ¼ teaspoon cream of tartar

For the Espresso Buttercream Filling:

- ½ cup (1 stick) unsalted butter, softened
- 1 ¼ cups (150g) powdered sugar
- 1 tablespoon finely ground espresso beans or instant espresso powder
- 1 tablespoon milk or heavy cream
- ½ teaspoon vanilla extract

Instructions:

1. **Prepare the Baking Sheets:**
   - Line two baking sheets with parchment paper or silicone baking mats.
   - If you have a macaron template, place it under the parchment paper to help guide your piping.
2. **Prepare the Dry Ingredients:**
   - In a medium bowl, sift together the almond flour and powdered sugar. Set aside.
3. **Whip the Egg Whites:**
   - In a clean, dry bowl, whip the egg whites with a hand mixer or stand mixer on medium speed until they become frothy.
   - Add the cream of tartar and continue to whip until soft peaks form.
   - Gradually add the granulated sugar while continuing to whip until stiff, glossy peaks form.
   - Gently fold in the espresso powder or finely ground espresso beans.
4. **Combine and Fold:**
   - Gently fold the sifted almond flour and powdered sugar mixture into the whipped egg whites in three parts. Use a spatula and fold until the batter flows slowly off the spatula in ribbons. Be careful not to overmix; the batter should be smooth and slightly glossy.
5. **Pipe the Macarons:**
   - Transfer the batter to a piping bag fitted with a round tip (about ¼ inch).
   - Pipe small rounds (about 1 ¼ inch) onto the prepared baking sheets, spacing them about 1 inch apart.

- Tap the baking sheets gently on the counter to release any air bubbles.
6. **Rest the Macarons:**
    - Let the piped macarons sit at room temperature for 30-60 minutes, or until the tops form a dry skin that doesn't stick to your finger when touched.
7. **Bake:**
    - Preheat your oven to 300°F (150°C).
    - Bake the macarons for 15-18 minutes, or until they are set and easily lift off the parchment paper. Avoid overbaking as they can become dry.
8. **Cool:**
    - Allow the macarons to cool completely on the baking sheets before removing them.
9. **Prepare the Espresso Buttercream Filling:**
    - In a medium bowl, beat the softened butter until creamy.
    - Gradually add the powdered sugar, beating until smooth.
    - Mix in the espresso powder, milk, and vanilla extract until well combined.
    - Adjust the consistency with additional milk if necessary.
10. **Assemble the Macarons:**
    - Pair up the macaron shells of similar size.
    - Pipe or spread a small amount of espresso buttercream onto the flat side of one shell.
    - Top with another shell, pressing gently to create a sandwich.
11. **Mature the Macarons:**
    - For best flavor and texture, let the assembled macarons mature in the refrigerator for at least 24 hours. Allow them to come to room temperature before serving.

Enjoy your homemade Espresso Macarons with a cup of coffee or as a special treat anytime!

Poppy Seed Lemon Muffins

Ingredients:

For the Muffins:

- 1 ½ cups all-purpose flour
- ½ cup granulated sugar
- 2 tablespoons poppy seeds
- 2 teaspoons baking powder
- ¼ teaspoon baking soda
- ¼ teaspoon salt
- ¼ cup unsalted butter, melted
- 1 large egg
- 1 cup buttermilk (or substitute with 1 cup milk + 1 tablespoon lemon juice, let sit for 5 minutes)
- 2 tablespoons lemon zest (about 1-2 lemons)
- 2 tablespoons freshly squeezed lemon juice

For the Lemon Glaze (Optional):

- ½ cup powdered sugar
- 2-3 tablespoons lemon juice

Instructions:

1. **Preheat Oven:**
   - Preheat your oven to 375°F (190°C).
   - Line a muffin tin with paper liners or lightly grease it.
2. **Prepare Dry Ingredients:**
   - In a large bowl, whisk together the flour, sugar, poppy seeds, baking powder, baking soda, and salt.
3. **Mix Wet Ingredients:**
   - In a separate bowl, combine the melted butter, egg, buttermilk, lemon zest, and lemon juice. Whisk until well combined.
4. **Combine Ingredients:**
   - Pour the wet ingredients into the dry ingredients and stir gently until just combined. Be careful not to overmix; a few lumps are okay.
5. **Fill Muffin Tins:**
   - Divide the batter evenly among the muffin cups, filling each about ¾ full.
6. **Bake:**
   - Bake for 18-22 minutes, or until a toothpick inserted into the center of a muffin comes out clean.
   - Let the muffins cool in the pan for about 5 minutes, then transfer to a wire rack to cool completely.
7. **Prepare Lemon Glaze (Optional):**

        - While the muffins are cooling, whisk together the powdered sugar and lemon juice in a small bowl until smooth.
        - Drizzle the glaze over the cooled muffins.
8. **Serve:**
        - Enjoy your Poppy Seed Lemon Muffins as a delightful breakfast or snack!

These muffins are a perfect blend of sweet and tangy, with a hint of crunch from the poppy seeds. They also keep well for a few days, making them a great make-ahead option. Enjoy!

Chocolate Dipped Pretzel Rods

Ingredients:

- 12-15 pretzel rods
- 1 cup semi-sweet chocolate chips (or dark/milk chocolate chips based on preference)
- 1 tablespoon coconut oil or vegetable oil (optional, for smoother melting)
- Assorted toppings (e.g., sprinkles, crushed nuts, crushed candy canes, sea salt, mini marshmallows, etc.)

Instructions:

1. **Prepare the Pretzels:**
    - Lay out the pretzel rods on a parchment-lined baking sheet or a large plate.
2. **Melt the Chocolate:**
    - **Microwave Method:** Place the chocolate chips and coconut oil (if using) in a microwave-safe bowl. Microwave in 30-second intervals, stirring between each interval, until the chocolate is fully melted and smooth.
    - **Double Boiler Method:** Place the chocolate chips and coconut oil in a heatproof bowl over a pot of simmering water (make sure the bowl does not touch the water). Stir occasionally until melted and smooth.
3. **Dip the Pretzels:**
    - Hold each pretzel rod by one end and dip it into the melted chocolate, covering about 2/3 of the pretzel.
    - Gently tap the pretzel rod against the side of the bowl to remove excess chocolate.
4. **Add Toppings:**
    - Immediately sprinkle or dip the chocolate-covered part of the pretzel rod into your choice of toppings while the chocolate is still wet.
5. **Cool and Set:**
    - Place the dipped pretzel rods back on the parchment-lined baking sheet or plate.
    - Allow the chocolate to set completely. You can speed up the process by placing the pretzels in the refrigerator for about 15-20 minutes.
6. **Serve or Store:**
    - Once the chocolate has set, the pretzel rods are ready to enjoy.
    - Store any leftover pretzels in an airtight container at room temperature for up to 1 week, or in the refrigerator for up to 2 weeks.

Feel free to get creative with your toppings and experiment with different combinations. Enjoy your chocolate-dipped pretzel rods!

Pear Ginger Cake

Ingredients:

For the Cake:

- 1 ½ cups all-purpose flour
- 1 teaspoon baking powder
- ½ teaspoon baking soda
- ½ teaspoon salt
- 2 teaspoons ground ginger
- 1 teaspoon ground cinnamon
- ¼ teaspoon ground cloves (optional)
- ½ cup unsalted butter, softened
- ¾ cup granulated sugar
- 2 large eggs
- ½ cup molasses
- ¼ cup milk (whole or 2%)
- 2 ripe pears, peeled, cored, and diced (about 1 ½ cups)
- ¼ cup finely chopped crystallized ginger (optional)

For the Topping (Optional):

- 2 tablespoons granulated sugar
- ½ teaspoon ground cinnamon

Instructions:

1. **Preheat Oven:**
   - Preheat your oven to 350°F (175°C).
   - Grease and flour a 9-inch round cake pan, or line it with parchment paper.
2. **Prepare Dry Ingredients:**
   - In a medium bowl, whisk together the flour, baking powder, baking soda, salt, ground ginger, cinnamon, and cloves.
3. **Cream Butter and Sugar:**
   - In a large bowl, beat the softened butter and granulated sugar together until light and fluffy, about 3-4 minutes.
4. **Add Eggs and Molasses:**
   - Beat in the eggs one at a time, ensuring each is fully incorporated before adding the next.
   - Mix in the molasses until well combined.
5. **Combine Ingredients:**
   - Gradually add the dry ingredients to the butter mixture, alternating with the milk. Start and end with the dry ingredients, mixing just until combined.
   - Gently fold in the diced pears and crystallized ginger (if using).
6. **Pour and Bake:**
   - Pour the batter into the prepared cake pan, spreading it evenly.

- If using the topping, mix the granulated sugar and cinnamon together and sprinkle it over the top of the batter.
- Bake for 35-40 minutes, or until a toothpick inserted into the center comes out clean.

7. **Cool and Serve:**
    - Allow the cake to cool in the pan for about 10 minutes, then transfer it to a wire rack to cool completely.
    - Serve plain or with a dusting of powdered sugar, a dollop of whipped cream, or a scoop of vanilla ice cream.

Enjoy the delightful combination of pear and ginger in this moist, flavorful cake!

Cinnamon Streusel Coffee Cake

Ingredients:

For the Streusel Topping:

- ¾ cup all-purpose flour
- ½ cup granulated sugar
- ¼ cup packed brown sugar
- 1 teaspoon ground cinnamon
- ¼ teaspoon salt
- 6 tablespoons unsalted butter, cold and cut into small pieces

For the Cake:

- 1 ½ cups all-purpose flour
- 1 teaspoon baking powder
- ½ teaspoon baking soda
- ¼ teaspoon salt
- ½ cup unsalted butter, softened
- ½ cup granulated sugar
- ½ cup packed brown sugar
- 2 large eggs
- 1 cup sour cream (or Greek yogurt)
- 1 teaspoon vanilla extract

Optional Glaze:

- ½ cup powdered sugar
- 2-3 tablespoons milk or cream
- ¼ teaspoon vanilla extract

Instructions:

1. **Preheat Oven:**
   - Preheat your oven to 350°F (175°C).
   - Grease and flour a 9-inch round cake pan or a 9x9-inch square pan. You can also line the pan with parchment paper for easier removal.
2. **Prepare the Streusel Topping:**
   - In a medium bowl, combine the flour, granulated sugar, brown sugar, cinnamon, and salt.
   - Add the cold butter pieces. Using a pastry cutter, your fingers, or a fork, cut the butter into the mixture until it resembles coarse crumbs. Set aside.
3. **Prepare the Cake Batter:**
   - In a medium bowl, whisk together the flour, baking powder, baking soda, and salt.
   - In a large bowl, cream together the softened butter, granulated sugar, and brown sugar until light and fluffy.

- Beat in the eggs one at a time, ensuring each is fully incorporated before adding the next.
- Mix in the sour cream (or Greek yogurt) and vanilla extract until well combined.
- Gradually add the dry ingredients to the wet ingredients, mixing just until combined.

4. **Assemble the Cake:**
   - Pour half of the cake batter into the prepared pan, spreading it evenly.
   - Sprinkle half of the streusel topping over the batter.
   - Add the remaining batter on top, spreading it evenly.
   - Sprinkle the remaining streusel topping over the top of the batter.

5. **Bake:**
   - Bake for 35-40 minutes, or until a toothpick inserted into the center of the cake comes out clean.

6. **Cool and Glaze (Optional):**
   - Allow the cake to cool in the pan for about 10 minutes before transferring it to a wire rack to cool completely.
   - If you're adding a glaze, whisk together the powdered sugar, milk (or cream), and vanilla extract until smooth. Drizzle the glaze over the cooled cake.

7. **Serve:**
   - Slice and enjoy the cake warm or at room temperature.

This Cinnamon Streusel Coffee Cake is sure to be a hit with its buttery texture and sweet, spiced topping. Enjoy it with a cup of coffee or tea for a perfect treat!

S'mores Brownies

Ingredients:

For the Brownies:

- 1 cup (2 sticks) unsalted butter
- 1 cup granulated sugar
- 2 large eggs
- 1 teaspoon vanilla extract
- 1 cup all-purpose flour
- ½ cup unsweetened cocoa powder
- ¼ teaspoon salt
- ¼ teaspoon baking powder
- ½ cup chocolate chips or chunks (optional)

For the S'mores Topping:

- ½ cup graham cracker crumbs (about 4-5 graham crackers, crushed)
- 1 cup mini marshmallows or 12 large marshmallows
- ½ cup chocolate chips or chunks
- Optional: extra graham cracker crumbs for sprinkling

Instructions:

1. **Preheat Oven:**
    - Preheat your oven to 350°F (175°C).
    - Grease and flour an 8x8-inch baking pan or line it with parchment paper.
2. **Prepare the Brownie Batter:**
    - In a medium saucepan, melt the butter over medium heat. Remove from heat and let it cool slightly.
    - Stir in the granulated sugar, eggs, and vanilla extract until combined.
    - In a separate bowl, whisk together the flour, cocoa powder, salt, and baking powder.
    - Gradually add the dry ingredients to the wet ingredients, mixing until just combined.
    - Fold in the chocolate chips or chunks if using.
3. **Bake the Brownies:**
    - Pour the brownie batter into the prepared baking pan, spreading it evenly.
    - Bake for 20-25 minutes, or until a toothpick inserted into the center comes out with just a few moist crumbs. The brownies should be set around the edges but still soft in the center.
4. **Add the S'mores Topping:**
    - While the brownies are baking, prepare the s'mores topping.
    - Remove the brownies from the oven and sprinkle the graham cracker crumbs evenly over the top.
    - Sprinkle the chocolate chips or chunks over the graham crackers.

- Distribute the mini marshmallows (or large marshmallows cut into smaller pieces) evenly over the top.
5. **Finish Baking:**
    - Return the brownies to the oven and bake for an additional 10-12 minutes, or until the marshmallows are golden brown and the chocolate is melted.
6. **Cool and Serve:**
    - Allow the brownies to cool completely in the pan on a wire rack before cutting into squares.
    - If desired, sprinkle additional graham cracker crumbs over the top for extra texture and flavor.

Enjoy your homemade S'mores Brownies as a rich, gooey treat that brings together all the beloved flavors of a classic s'more in a fudgy brownie form!

Coconut Lime Bars

Ingredients:

For the Crust:

- 1 ½ cups graham cracker crumbs (about 12-14 graham crackers)
- ¼ cup granulated sugar
- ½ cup unsalted butter, melted

For the Filling:

- 1 can (14 ounces) sweetened condensed milk
- ½ cup freshly squeezed lime juice (about 4-5 limes)
- 1 tablespoon lime zest (about 2 limes)
- 1 cup shredded coconut (sweetened or unsweetened, based on preference)
- 2 large eggs

For the Topping (Optional):

- Additional shredded coconut for sprinkling
- Lime zest for garnish

Instructions:

1. **Preheat Oven:**
   - Preheat your oven to 350°F (175°C).
   - Grease and line an 8x8-inch baking pan with parchment paper, leaving some overhang for easy removal.
2. **Prepare the Crust:**
   - In a medium bowl, combine the graham cracker crumbs, granulated sugar, and melted butter. Mix until the crumbs are evenly coated and the mixture resembles wet sand.
   - Press the mixture evenly into the bottom of the prepared pan to form the crust.
3. **Bake the Crust:**
   - Bake the crust for 8-10 minutes, or until it is lightly golden. Remove from the oven and let it cool slightly.
4. **Prepare the Filling:**
   - In a large bowl, whisk together the sweetened condensed milk, lime juice, lime zest, and eggs until well combined.
   - Stir in the shredded coconut.
5. **Pour and Bake:**
   - Pour the filling over the slightly cooled crust and spread it evenly.
   - Bake for 20-25 minutes, or until the filling is set and the top is slightly golden. A toothpick inserted into the center should come out clean.
6. **Cool and Garnish:**
   - Allow the bars to cool completely in the pan on a wire rack.
   - Once cool, lift the bars out of the pan using the parchment paper overhang and cut into squares.

7. **Add Toppings (Optional):**
    - For extra texture and flavor, you can sprinkle additional shredded coconut and lime zest on top before serving.
8. **Serve:**
    - Enjoy your Coconut Lime Bars chilled or at room temperature. They are perfect for a refreshing dessert or a sweet treat with a tropical twist!

These bars offer a delightful balance of creamy coconut and tangy lime, making them a perfect summer dessert or a bright addition to any dessert spread.

Nutella Swirl Banana Bread

Ingredients:

For the Banana Bread:

- 1 ½ cups all-purpose flour
- 1 teaspoon baking powder
- ½ teaspoon baking soda
- ¼ teaspoon salt
- ¼ cup unsalted butter, softened
- ½ cup granulated sugar
- ¼ cup packed brown sugar
- 2 large eggs
- ½ cup sour cream or Greek yogurt
- 1 teaspoon vanilla extract
- 3 ripe bananas, mashed (about 1 ½ cups)

For the Nutella Swirl:

- ½ cup Nutella (chocolate-hazelnut spread)

Instructions:

1. **Preheat Oven:**
   - Preheat your oven to 350°F (175°C).
   - Grease and flour a 9x5-inch loaf pan or line it with parchment paper.
2. **Prepare Dry Ingredients:**
   - In a medium bowl, whisk together the flour, baking powder, baking soda, and salt. Set aside.
3. **Cream Butter and Sugars:**
   - In a large bowl, beat the softened butter, granulated sugar, and brown sugar together until light and fluffy, about 3-4 minutes.
4. **Add Wet Ingredients:**
   - Beat in the eggs one at a time, making sure each egg is fully incorporated before adding the next.
   - Mix in the sour cream (or Greek yogurt) and vanilla extract until smooth.
   - Stir in the mashed bananas until well combined.
5. **Combine Ingredients:**
   - Gradually add the dry ingredients to the wet ingredients, mixing until just combined. Be careful not to overmix.
6. **Prepare the Nutella Swirl:**
   - Gently fold about 2-3 tablespoons of Nutella into the batter. You want to create ribbons of Nutella, not fully mix it in.
7. **Assemble the Bread:**
   - Pour the batter into the prepared loaf pan.
   - Drop spoonfuls of the remaining Nutella on top of the batter. Use a knife or a skewer to swirl the Nutella into the batter, creating a marbled effect.
8. **Bake:**

- Bake for 55-65 minutes, or until a toothpick inserted into the center of the bread comes out clean. The top should be golden brown and firm to the touch.
9. **Cool:**
    - Allow the bread to cool in the pan for about 10 minutes before transferring it to a wire rack to cool completely.
10. **Serve:**
    - Slice and enjoy! The Nutella Swirl Banana Bread is delicious on its own, or you can enjoy it with a cup of coffee or tea.

This Nutella Swirl Banana Bread is a delightful fusion of banana bread and chocolate-hazelnut spread, perfect for breakfast, a snack, or dessert. Enjoy the rich, chocolatey swirl with each bite!

Berry Crumble Bars

Ingredients:

For the Crust and Crumble Topping:

- 1 ½ cups all-purpose flour
- 1 cup granulated sugar
- ½ teaspoon baking powder
- ¼ teaspoon salt
- ½ cup unsalted butter, cold and cut into small pieces

For the Berry Filling:

- 2 cups fresh or frozen mixed berries (such as strawberries, blueberries, raspberries, blackberries)
- ¼ cup granulated sugar (adjust based on the sweetness of the berries)
- 1 tablespoon lemon juice
- 2 tablespoons cornstarch

Instructions:

1. **Preheat Oven:**
   - Preheat your oven to 350°F (175°C).
   - Grease and line an 8x8-inch baking pan with parchment paper, leaving some overhang for easy removal.
2. **Prepare the Crust and Crumble Topping:**
   - In a medium bowl, whisk together the flour, sugar, baking powder, and salt.
   - Cut in the cold butter using a pastry cutter or your fingers until the mixture resembles coarse crumbs. Reserve 1 cup of this mixture for the crumble topping.
   - Press the remaining mixture evenly into the bottom of the prepared pan to form the crust.
3. **Prepare the Berry Filling:**
   - In a medium saucepan, combine the berries, sugar, lemon juice, and cornstarch.
   - Cook over medium heat, stirring constantly, until the mixture starts to thicken and bubble, about 5-7 minutes.
   - Remove from heat and let it cool slightly.
4. **Assemble the Bars:**
   - Spread the berry filling evenly over the pre-baked crust.
   - Sprinkle the reserved crumble mixture evenly over the berry filling.
5. **Bake:**
   - Bake for 35-40 minutes, or until the topping is golden brown and the filling is bubbly.
6. **Cool and Slice:**
   - Allow the bars to cool completely in the pan on a wire rack before lifting them out and cutting into squares.
7. **Serve:**
   - Enjoy your Berry Crumble Bars as a sweet treat or dessert. They're delicious on their own or with a dollop of whipped cream or a scoop of vanilla ice cream.

These Berry Crumble Bars are a versatile and delightful way to enjoy the flavors of fresh or frozen berries. They're perfect for potlucks, family gatherings, or just a simple treat to brighten your day!

Toffee Pecan Cookies

Ingredients:

- 1 cup (2 sticks) unsalted butter, softened
- ¾ cup granulated sugar

- ¾ cup packed brown sugar
- 1 large egg
- 1 teaspoon vanilla extract
- 2 ¼ cups all-purpose flour
- 1 teaspoon baking soda
- ¼ teaspoon salt
- 1 cup toffee bits (like Heath Bar bits or Skor bits)
- 1 cup chopped pecans

Instructions:

1. **Preheat Oven:**
   - Preheat your oven to 350°F (175°C).
   - Line baking sheets with parchment paper or silicone baking mats.
2. **Cream Butter and Sugars:**
   - In a large bowl, cream together the softened butter, granulated sugar, and brown sugar until light and fluffy, about 2-3 minutes.
3. **Add Egg and Vanilla:**
   - Beat in the egg and vanilla extract until well combined.
4. **Combine Dry Ingredients:**
   - In a separate bowl, whisk together the flour, baking soda, and salt.
5. **Mix Dry and Wet Ingredients:**
   - Gradually add the dry ingredients to the wet ingredients, mixing until just combined.
6. **Fold in Toffee Bits and Pecans:**
   - Gently fold in the toffee bits and chopped pecans until evenly distributed throughout the dough.
7. **Scoop Dough:**
   - Using a cookie scoop or tablespoon, drop rounded balls of dough onto the prepared baking sheets, spacing them about 2 inches apart.
8. **Bake:**
   - Bake for 10-12 minutes, or until the edges are golden brown and the centers are set. The cookies will continue to cook slightly after being removed from the oven.
9. **Cool:**
   - Allow the cookies to cool on the baking sheets for about 5 minutes before transferring them to a wire rack to cool completely.
10. **Serve:**
    - Enjoy your Toffee Pecan Cookies with a glass of milk or a cup of coffee. They're perfect for a sweet treat or dessert!

These Toffee Pecan Cookies offer a delightful mix of sweet toffee, crunchy pecans, and buttery cookie goodness. They're sure to be a favorite among family and friends!

Chocolate Raspberry Tart

Ingredients:

For the Tart Crust:

- 1 ½ cups all-purpose flour
- ¼ cup granulated sugar
- ¼ teaspoon salt
- ½ cup (1 stick) unsalted butter, cold and cut into small pieces
- 1 large egg yolk
- 2-3 tablespoons ice water

For the Chocolate Ganache Filling:

- 8 ounces semi-sweet or bittersweet chocolate, chopped
- 1 cup heavy cream
- 2 tablespoons unsalted butter
- 1 teaspoon vanilla extract

For the Raspberry Layer:

- 1 cup fresh raspberries
- 2 tablespoons granulated sugar (optional, depending on the sweetness of the raspberries)

For Garnish (Optional):

- Fresh raspberries
- Mint leaves
- Shaved chocolate

Instructions:

1. **Prepare the Tart Crust:**
   - In a food processor, combine the flour, sugar, and salt. Pulse to mix.
   - Add the cold butter and pulse until the mixture resembles coarse crumbs.
   - Add the egg yolk and pulse until combined.
   - Gradually add the ice water, one tablespoon at a time, until the dough starts to come together.
   - Turn the dough out onto a floured surface and knead it a few times to bring it together. Flatten into a disk, wrap in plastic wrap, and refrigerate for at least 30 minutes.
2. **Preheat Oven:**
   - Preheat your oven to 350°F (175°C).
3. **Roll Out the Dough:**
   - On a floured surface, roll out the dough to fit a 9-inch tart pan with a removable bottom. Carefully transfer the dough to the tart pan, pressing it into the edges. Trim any excess dough.
   - Line the dough with parchment paper and fill with pie weights or dried beans.
4. **Bake the Crust:**

        - Bake the crust for 15 minutes. Remove the parchment paper and weights, and bake for an additional 10-12 minutes, or until the crust is golden brown.
        - Allow the crust to cool completely.
5. **Prepare the Chocolate Ganache:**
        - Place the chopped chocolate in a heatproof bowl.
        - In a small saucepan, heat the heavy cream until just boiling. Pour the hot cream over the chocolate and let it sit for 2-3 minutes.
        - Stir until the chocolate is completely melted and smooth. Add the butter and vanilla extract, and stir until combined.
6. **Assemble the Tart:**
        - Pour the chocolate ganache into the cooled tart crust, spreading it evenly.
        - Arrange the fresh raspberries on top of the ganache. If desired, sprinkle the raspberries with granulated sugar for a bit of extra sweetness.
7. **Chill:**
        - Refrigerate the tart for at least 2 hours, or until the ganache is set.
8. **Garnish and Serve:**
        - Before serving, garnish with additional fresh raspberries, mint leaves, and shaved chocolate if desired.
        - Remove the tart from the pan and slice into wedges to serve.

This Chocolate Raspberry Tart is a perfect blend of rich chocolate and tart raspberries, with a buttery crust that ties everything together. Enjoy this elegant dessert for any special occasion or as a delightful treat!

Apple Streusel Muffins

Ingredients:

For the Muffins:

- 2 cups all-purpose flour
- ½ cup granulated sugar
- ¼ cup packed brown sugar
- 1 tablespoon baking powder
- ½ teaspoon baking soda
- ½ teaspoon salt
- 1 teaspoon ground cinnamon
- ½ teaspoon ground nutmeg
- ½ cup unsalted butter, melted
- 1 large egg
- 1 cup buttermilk (or milk with 1 tablespoon lemon juice or vinegar)
- 1 teaspoon vanilla extract
- 1 ½ cups peeled and diced apples (about 1-2 medium apples)

For the Streusel Topping:

- ⅓ cup all-purpose flour
- ¼ cup granulated sugar
- ¼ cup packed brown sugar
- ½ teaspoon ground cinnamon
- ¼ cup unsalted butter, cold and cut into small pieces

Instructions:

1. **Preheat Oven:**
   - Preheat your oven to 375°F (190°C).
   - Line a 12-cup muffin tin with paper liners or lightly grease the cups.
2. **Prepare the Streusel Topping:**
   - In a small bowl, combine the flour, granulated sugar, brown sugar, and cinnamon.
   - Add the cold butter pieces and use a pastry cutter or your fingers to mix until the mixture resembles coarse crumbs. Set aside.
3. **Prepare the Muffin Batter:**
   - In a large bowl, whisk together the flour, granulated sugar, brown sugar, baking powder, baking soda, salt, cinnamon, and nutmeg.
   - In another bowl, mix together the melted butter, egg, buttermilk, and vanilla extract until well combined.
   - Pour the wet ingredients into the dry ingredients and stir until just combined. Be careful not to overmix.
   - Gently fold in the diced apples.
4. **Fill Muffin Tin:**
   - Divide the muffin batter evenly among the 12 muffin cups, filling each about 2/3 full.
5. **Add Streusel Topping:**
   - Sprinkle the streusel topping evenly over the muffin batter.
6. **Bake:**

        - Bake for 18-22 minutes, or until a toothpick inserted into the center of a muffin comes out clean and the tops are golden brown.
7. **Cool:**
        - Allow the muffins to cool in the tin for about 5 minutes before transferring them to a wire rack to cool completely.
8. **Serve:**
        - Enjoy your Apple Streusel Muffins warm or at room temperature. They're great on their own or with a cup of coffee or tea.

These Apple Streusel Muffins are a delightful combination of tender apple-studded muffin with a crisp, buttery streusel topping. They're perfect for adding a bit of warmth and comfort to your day!

Peanut Butter Cupcakes

Ingredients:

For the Cupcakes:

- 1 ½ cups all-purpose flour
- 1 cup granulated sugar
- ½ teaspoon baking powder
- ½ teaspoon baking soda
- ¼ teaspoon salt
- ½ cup unsalted butter, softened
- ½ cup creamy peanut butter
- 2 large eggs
- ½ cup milk (whole or 2%)
- ½ teaspoon vanilla extract

For the Peanut Butter Frosting:

- ½ cup unsalted butter, softened
- ½ cup creamy peanut butter
- 2 cups powdered sugar
- 2-3 tablespoons milk (whole or 2%)
- ½ teaspoon vanilla extract

Optional Garnish:

- Mini peanut butter cups
- Crushed peanuts

Instructions:

1. **Preheat Oven:**
    - Preheat your oven to 350°F (175°C).
    - Line a 12-cup muffin tin with paper liners.
2. **Prepare the Cupcake Batter:**
    - In a medium bowl, whisk together the flour, sugar, baking powder, baking soda, and salt.
    - In a large bowl, beat the softened butter and peanut butter together until creamy and well combined.
    - Add the eggs one at a time, beating well after each addition.
    - Mix in the vanilla extract.
    - Gradually add the dry ingredients to the butter mixture, alternating with the milk, beginning and ending with the dry ingredients. Mix until just combined.
3. **Fill and Bake:**
    - Divide the batter evenly among the 12 cupcake liners, filling each about 2/3 full.
    - Bake for 18-20 minutes, or until a toothpick inserted into the center of a cupcake comes out clean.
4. **Cool:**
    - Allow the cupcakes to cool in the tin for about 5 minutes, then transfer them to a wire rack to cool completely before frosting.

5. **Prepare the Peanut Butter Frosting:**
    - In a medium bowl, beat the softened butter and peanut butter together until smooth and creamy.
    - Gradually add the powdered sugar, mixing on low speed until combined.
    - Add the milk, one tablespoon at a time, until the frosting reaches your desired consistency.
    - Mix in the vanilla extract.
6. **Frost the Cupcakes:**
    - Once the cupcakes are completely cool, frost them with the peanut butter frosting using a piping bag or a spatula.
    - If desired, garnish with mini peanut butter cups or crushed peanuts.
7. **Serve:**
    - Enjoy your Peanut Butter Cupcakes as a sweet treat. They're perfect for parties, special occasions, or just a delicious everyday indulgence!

These Peanut Butter Cupcakes are a peanut butter lover's dream, combining the rich flavor of peanut butter with a light and fluffy cupcake base. The creamy frosting and optional garnishes make them an extra special treat!

Chai Spice Cake

Ingredients:

For the Cake:

- 2 ½ cups all-purpose flour
- 1 ½ teaspoons baking powder
- ½ teaspoon baking soda
- ½ teaspoon salt
- 1 tablespoon ground cinnamon
- 1 teaspoon ground cardamom
- 1 teaspoon ground ginger
- ¼ teaspoon ground cloves
- 1 cup (2 sticks) unsalted butter, softened
- 1 cup granulated sugar
- ½ cup packed brown sugar
- 3 large eggs
- 1 cup buttermilk (or milk with 1 tablespoon lemon juice or vinegar)
- 1 teaspoon vanilla extract

For the Chai Spice Frosting:

- ½ cup (1 stick) unsalted butter, softened
- 4 cups powdered sugar
- 2 tablespoons heavy cream (or milk)
- 1 teaspoon vanilla extract
- 1 teaspoon ground cinnamon
- ½ teaspoon ground cardamom
- ¼ teaspoon ground ginger
- ¼ teaspoon ground cloves

Optional Garnish:

- Ground cinnamon
- Crystallized ginger pieces
- Chopped nuts (e.g., pecans or walnuts)

Instructions:

1. **Preheat Oven:**
   - Preheat your oven to 350°F (175°C).
   - Grease and flour two 8-inch round cake pans or line them with parchment paper.
2. **Prepare the Dry Ingredients:**
   - In a medium bowl, whisk together the flour, baking powder, baking soda, salt, cinnamon, cardamom, ginger, and cloves. Set aside.
3. **Cream Butter and Sugars:**
   - In a large bowl, cream together the softened butter, granulated sugar, and brown sugar until light and fluffy, about 3-4 minutes.
4. **Add Eggs and Vanilla:**

- Beat in the eggs one at a time, making sure each is fully incorporated before adding the next.
- Mix in the vanilla extract.

5. **Combine Dry and Wet Ingredients:**
   - Gradually add the dry ingredients to the wet ingredients, alternating with the buttermilk. Begin and end with the dry ingredients. Mix until just combined.

6. **Bake:**
   - Divide the batter evenly between the prepared cake pans.
   - Bake for 25-30 minutes, or until a toothpick inserted into the center of the cakes comes out clean and the tops are golden brown.

7. **Cool:**
   - Allow the cakes to cool in the pans for about 10 minutes before transferring them to a wire rack to cool completely.

8. **Prepare the Chai Spice Frosting:**
   - In a medium bowl, beat the softened butter until creamy.
   - Gradually add the powdered sugar, mixing on low speed until combined.
   - Add the heavy cream (or milk) and vanilla extract, and beat until smooth and spreadable.
   - Mix in the cinnamon, cardamom, ginger, and cloves until evenly distributed.

9. **Frost the Cake:**
   - Once the cakes are completely cool, spread a layer of frosting on top of one cake layer.
   - Place the second cake layer on top and frost the top and sides of the cake with the remaining frosting.

10. **Garnish and Serve:**
    - If desired, sprinkle a bit of ground cinnamon over the top or add chopped nuts and crystallized ginger pieces for extra texture and flavor.
    - Slice and enjoy your Chai Spice Cake with a cup of tea or coffee.

This Chai Spice Cake is perfect for those who love warm, comforting spices. It's great for fall gatherings, holiday celebrations, or any time you want a delightful, spiced treat!

Tiramisu Cheesecake

Ingredients:

For the Crust:

- 1 ½ cups graham cracker crumbs
- ¼ cup granulated sugar
- ¼ cup unsalted butter, melted

For the Cheesecake Filling:

- 3 (8-ounce) packages cream cheese, softened
- 1 cup granulated sugar
- 1 teaspoon vanilla extract
- 3 large eggs
- 1 cup sour cream
- ½ cup heavy cream
- 1 cup mascarpone cheese, softened
- 1 cup brewed espresso or strong coffee, cooled
- 2 tablespoons coffee liqueur (optional)
- ¼ cup all-purpose flour

For the Topping:

- ¼ cup unsweetened cocoa powder
- Optional: Shaved chocolate or chocolate curls

Instructions:

1. **Preheat Oven:**
   - Preheat your oven to 325°F (160°C).
   - Grease a 9-inch springform pan or line it with parchment paper. Wrap the outside of the pan with aluminum foil to prevent leaks.
2. **Prepare the Crust:**
   - In a medium bowl, combine the graham cracker crumbs, granulated sugar, and melted butter. Mix until the crumbs are evenly coated and resemble wet sand.
   - Press the mixture firmly into the bottom of the prepared pan to form an even crust.
   - Bake the crust for 10 minutes, then remove from the oven and let it cool slightly.
3. **Prepare the Cheesecake Filling:**
   - In a large bowl, beat the cream cheese until smooth and creamy.
   - Add the sugar and vanilla extract, and beat until well combined.
   - Add the eggs one at a time, beating well after each addition.
   - Mix in the sour cream and heavy cream until smooth.
   - Beat in the mascarpone cheese until incorporated.
   - Gradually add the cooled espresso or coffee and coffee liqueur (if using), mixing until well combined.
   - Stir in the flour until just incorporated.

4. **Assemble the Cheesecake:**
    - Pour half of the cheesecake batter over the pre-baked crust and smooth the top.
    - Dip ladyfingers in the cooled espresso or coffee, one at a time, and layer them over the cheesecake batter.
    - Pour the remaining cheesecake batter over the ladyfingers and smooth the top.
5. **Bake:**
    - Place the springform pan in a large roasting pan and add hot water to the roasting pan to create a water bath (about 1 inch of water).
    - Bake the cheesecake for 55-65 minutes, or until the edges are set but the center is still slightly jiggly. The cheesecake will firm up as it cools.
6. **Cool:**
    - Turn off the oven and crack the oven door slightly. Let the cheesecake cool in the oven for 1 hour.
    - Remove the cheesecake from the water bath and refrigerate for at least 4 hours, or preferably overnight, to fully set.
7. **Prepare the Topping:**
    - Before serving, dust the top of the cheesecake with unsweetened cocoa powder using a fine sieve.
    - Garnish with shaved chocolate or chocolate curls, if desired.
8. **Serve:**
    - Remove the cheesecake from the springform pan and slice. Enjoy your Tiramisu Cheesecake chilled!

This Tiramisu Cheesecake is a perfect blend of creamy cheesecake and the classic flavors of tiramisu. It's a showstopper for any dessert table and will surely impress your guests!

Hazelnut Mocha Brownies

Ingredients:

For the Brownies:

- ½ cup (1 stick) unsalted butter
- 1 cup granulated sugar
- 2 large eggs
- 1 teaspoon vanilla extract
- ¼ cup brewed espresso or strong coffee, cooled
- ½ cup unsweetened cocoa powder
- 1 cup all-purpose flour
- ¼ teaspoon salt
- ½ teaspoon baking powder
- 1 cup chopped hazelnuts (toasted if desired)

For the Ganache (Optional):

- ½ cup heavy cream
- 4 ounces semi-sweet chocolate, chopped

For Garnish (Optional):

- Additional chopped hazelnuts
- Sea salt

Instructions:

1. **Preheat Oven:**
   - Preheat your oven to 350°F (175°C).
   - Grease and line an 8x8-inch baking pan with parchment paper, leaving an overhang for easy removal.
2. **Prepare the Brownie Batter:**
   - In a medium saucepan, melt the butter over low heat.
   - Remove from heat and stir in the granulated sugar, eggs, and vanilla extract until well combined.
   - Mix in the brewed espresso or coffee.
   - Stir in the cocoa powder until smooth.
   - Add the flour, salt, and baking powder. Mix until just combined.
   - Fold in the chopped hazelnuts.
3. **Bake:**
   - Pour the brownie batter into the prepared baking pan and spread it evenly.
   - Bake for 25-30 minutes, or until a toothpick inserted into the center comes out with just a few moist crumbs.
4. **Cool:**
   - Allow the brownies to cool completely in the pan on a wire rack before cutting into squares.
5. **Prepare the Ganache (Optional):**

- 6. **Garnish and Serve:**
        - While the brownies are cooling, heat the heavy cream in a small saucepan until it begins to simmer.
        - Remove from heat and add the chopped chocolate. Let it sit for 2 minutes, then stir until smooth and glossy.
        - Once the brownies are completely cool, spread the ganache evenly over the top.
7. **Garnish and Serve:**
    - If desired, sprinkle additional chopped hazelnuts and a pinch of sea salt over the ganache for extra flavor and texture.
    - Cut the brownies into squares and enjoy!

These Hazelnut Mocha Brownies offer a delicious blend of rich chocolate, nutty hazelnuts, and a hint of coffee flavor. They're perfect for a special treat or a delightful dessert!

Lemon Ricotta Pound Cake

Ingredients:

For the Cake:

- 1 ½ cups all-purpose flour
- 1 ½ teaspoons baking powder
- ¼ teaspoon salt
- ½ cup (1 stick) unsalted butter, softened
- 1 cup granulated sugar
- 3 large eggs
- 1 cup ricotta cheese (whole milk or part-skim)
- 2 tablespoons lemon zest (about 2 lemons)
- ¼ cup fresh lemon juice (about 1 lemon)
- 1 teaspoon vanilla extract

For the Lemon Glaze:

- 1 cup powdered sugar
- 2-3 tablespoons fresh lemon juice

Optional Garnish:

- Lemon zest
- Fresh berries

Instructions:

1. **Preheat Oven:**
    - Preheat your oven to 350°F (175°C).
    - Grease and flour a 9x5-inch loaf pan or line it with parchment paper, leaving an overhang for easy removal.
2. **Prepare the Dry Ingredients:**
    - In a medium bowl, whisk together the flour, baking powder, and salt. Set aside.
3. **Cream Butter and Sugar:**
    - In a large bowl, cream together the softened butter and granulated sugar until light and fluffy, about 3-4 minutes.
4. **Add Eggs and Ricotta:**
    - Beat in the eggs one at a time, ensuring each egg is fully incorporated before adding the next.
    - Mix in the ricotta cheese until well combined.
5. **Mix in Lemon and Vanilla:**
    - Stir in the lemon zest, lemon juice, and vanilla extract.
6. **Combine Ingredients:**
    - Gradually add the dry ingredients to the wet ingredients, mixing until just combined. Be careful not to overmix.
7. **Pour and Bake:**
    - Pour the batter into the prepared loaf pan and smooth the top with a spatula.

- Bake for 50-60 minutes, or until a toothpick inserted into the center of the cake comes out clean and the top is golden brown.
8. **Cool:**
    - Allow the cake to cool in the pan for 10 minutes before transferring it to a wire rack to cool completely.
9. **Prepare the Lemon Glaze:**
    - In a small bowl, whisk together the powdered sugar and lemon juice until smooth. Adjust the consistency with more lemon juice if necessary—it should be pourable but thick enough to coat the cake.
10. **Glaze and Garnish:**
    - Once the cake is completely cooled, drizzle the lemon glaze over the top.
    - Garnish with additional lemon zest or fresh berries if desired.
11. **Serve:**
    - Slice and enjoy your Lemon Ricotta Pound Cake with a cup of tea or coffee, or simply as a refreshing and tangy dessert.

This Lemon Ricotta Pound Cake is wonderfully moist with a subtle lemon flavor and a hint of creaminess from the ricotta. It's perfect for any occasion and is sure to be a hit with lemon lovers!

Gingerbread Bundt Cake

Ingredients:

For the Cake:

- 2 ½ cups all-purpose flour
- 1 teaspoon baking powder
- 1 teaspoon baking soda
- 1 teaspoon ground cinnamon
- 1 teaspoon ground ginger
- ¼ teaspoon ground cloves
- ¼ teaspoon salt
- ½ cup (1 stick) unsalted butter, softened
- ½ cup dark brown sugar, packed
- ½ cup granulated sugar
- 2 large eggs
- 1 cup molasses (unsulfured)
- 1 cup buttermilk (or milk with 1 tablespoon lemon juice or vinegar)
- 1 teaspoon vanilla extract

For the Glaze:

- 1 cup powdered sugar
- 2-3 tablespoons milk (or heavy cream)
- ½ teaspoon ground cinnamon (optional)

Optional Garnish:

- Whipped cream or crème fraîche
- Candied ginger pieces

Instructions:

1. **Preheat Oven:**
    - Preheat your oven to 350°F (175°C).
    - Grease and flour a 10-cup Bundt pan or spray it with non-stick baking spray.
2. **Prepare Dry Ingredients:**
    - In a medium bowl, whisk together the flour, baking powder, baking soda, cinnamon, ginger, cloves, and salt. Set aside.
3. **Cream Butter and Sugars:**
    - In a large bowl, cream together the softened butter, brown sugar, and granulated sugar until light and fluffy, about 3-4 minutes.
4. **Add Eggs and Molasses:**
    - Beat in the eggs one at a time, ensuring each egg is fully incorporated before adding the next.
    - Mix in the molasses until well combined.
5. **Combine Wet and Dry Ingredients:**

- Gradually add the dry ingredients to the wet ingredients, alternating with the buttermilk. Begin and end with the dry ingredients. Mix until just combined.
- Stir in the vanilla extract.
6. **Pour and Bake:**
    - Pour the batter into the prepared Bundt pan and smooth the top with a spatula.
    - Bake for 50-60 minutes, or until a toothpick inserted into the center of the cake comes out clean and the cake is golden brown.
7. **Cool:**
    - Allow the cake to cool in the pan for 15 minutes before transferring it to a wire rack to cool completely.
8. **Prepare the Glaze:**
    - In a small bowl, whisk together the powdered sugar and milk until smooth. Adjust the consistency with more milk if necessary.
    - If desired, mix in ground cinnamon for an extra hint of spice.
9. **Glaze and Garnish:**
    - Once the cake is completely cooled, drizzle the glaze over the top of the cake.
    - Garnish with whipped cream or crème fraîche and candied ginger pieces if desired.
10. **Serve:**
    - Slice and enjoy your Gingerbread Bundt Cake with a cup of tea or coffee, or as a delightful dessert for any occasion.

This Gingerbread Bundt Cake is beautifully spiced and incredibly moist, making it a perfect choice for festive gatherings or any time you want a comforting treat.

Peppermint Meringue Cookies

Ingredients:

For the Meringue Cookies:

- 4 large egg whites, at room temperature
- 1/4 teaspoon cream of tartar
- 1 cup granulated sugar
- 1/2 teaspoon pure vanilla extract
- 1/2 teaspoon pure peppermint extract
- 1/4 teaspoon red or pink gel food coloring (optional, for a festive touch)
- 1/2 cup crushed peppermint candies or candy canes (for garnish)

For Garnish (Optional):

- Additional crushed peppermint candies or candy canes

Instructions:

1. **Preheat Oven:**
    - Preheat your oven to 200°F (95°C).
    - Line two baking sheets with parchment paper or silicone baking mats.
2. **Prepare the Meringue:**
    - In a large, clean bowl, using an electric mixer or stand mixer fitted with a whisk attachment, beat the egg whites and cream of tartar on medium speed until soft peaks form.
    - Gradually add the granulated sugar, about 1 tablespoon at a time, beating on high speed until stiff, glossy peaks form and the sugar is completely dissolved. This should take about 5-7 minutes.
    - Gently fold in the vanilla extract, peppermint extract, and gel food coloring (if using) until evenly distributed.
3. **Pipe the Meringues:**
    - Transfer the meringue mixture to a piping bag fitted with a star tip or plain round tip.
    - Pipe small mounds or swirls of meringue onto the prepared baking sheets, spacing them about 1 inch apart. You can also use a spoon to dollop the meringue if you prefer.
4. **Bake:**
    - Bake the meringues in the preheated oven for 1 1/2 to 2 hours, or until they are crisp and dry to the touch. The meringues should easily lift off the parchment paper without sticking.
    - Turn off the oven and let the meringues cool completely in the oven with the door slightly ajar.
5. **Garnish:**
    - Once the meringues are completely cooled, gently press a few crushed peppermint candies or candy canes onto the tops of each meringue.

6. **Store:**
    - Store the meringue cookies in an airtight container at room temperature. They will keep for up to 2 weeks.
7. **Serve:**
    - Enjoy your Peppermint Meringue Cookies as a light, festive treat. They pair wonderfully with hot cocoa or coffee and are a great addition to holiday cookie trays.

These Peppermint Meringue Cookies are crisp on the outside and airy on the inside, with a delightful peppermint flavor. They're perfect for adding a touch of holiday cheer to any occasion!

Chocolate Cherry Cheesecake

Ingredients:

For the Crust:

- 1 ½ cups chocolate cookie crumbs (e.g., Oreo or chocolate graham crackers)
- ¼ cup granulated sugar
- 6 tablespoons unsalted butter, melted

For the Cheesecake Filling:

- 4 (8-ounce) packages cream cheese, softened
- 1 cup granulated sugar
- 1 teaspoon vanilla extract
- 4 large eggs
- 1 cup sour cream
- 1 cup heavy cream
- 1 cup semi-sweet chocolate chips or chopped chocolate

For the Cherry Topping:

- 1 cup fresh or frozen cherries, pitted
- ¼ cup granulated sugar
- 1 tablespoon lemon juice
- 1 tablespoon cornstarch
- ½ cup water

Optional Garnish:

- Whipped cream
- Chocolate shavings or curls
- Fresh cherries

Instructions:

1. **Preheat Oven:**
   - Preheat your oven to 325°F (160°C).
   - Grease a 9-inch springform pan and line the bottom with parchment paper.
2. **Prepare the Crust:**
   - In a medium bowl, combine the chocolate cookie crumbs, granulated sugar, and melted butter. Mix until the crumbs are evenly coated.
   - Press the mixture firmly into the bottom of the prepared springform pan to form an even crust.
   - Bake for 10 minutes, then remove from the oven and let cool while you prepare the filling.
3. **Prepare the Cheesecake Filling:**

- In a microwave-safe bowl, melt the semi-sweet chocolate in the microwave in 30-second intervals, stirring after each interval until smooth. Let it cool slightly.
- In a large bowl, beat the softened cream cheese until smooth and creamy.
- Add the granulated sugar and vanilla extract, and beat until well combined.
- Add the eggs one at a time, beating well after each addition.
- Mix in the sour cream and heavy cream until smooth.
- Gradually fold in the melted chocolate until evenly incorporated.

4. **Assemble and Bake:**
    - Pour the cheesecake batter over the cooled crust in the springform pan.
    - Smooth the top with a spatula.
    - Bake for 55-65 minutes, or until the edges are set but the center is still slightly jiggly. The cheesecake will firm up as it cools.
    - Turn off the oven and crack the oven door slightly. Let the cheesecake cool in the oven for 1 hour before transferring it to the refrigerator.
    - Refrigerate the cheesecake for at least 4 hours, or preferably overnight.
5. **Prepare the Cherry Topping:**
    - In a medium saucepan, combine the cherries, granulated sugar, lemon juice, cornstarch, and water.
    - Cook over medium heat, stirring frequently, until the mixture thickens and becomes glossy, about 5-7 minutes.
    - Remove from heat and let cool completely.
6. **Top the Cheesecake:**
    - Once the cheesecake is fully chilled, spread the cherry topping evenly over the top.
7. **Garnish and Serve:**
    - If desired, garnish with whipped cream, chocolate shavings or curls, and fresh cherries.
    - Slice and serve your Chocolate Cherry Cheesecake. Enjoy!

This Chocolate Cherry Cheesecake is a luxurious dessert that combines the richness of chocolate with the bright, tart flavor of cherries, creating a perfect balance of flavors and textures. It's sure to impress your guests and make any occasion special!

Orange Almond Biscotti

Ingredients:

For the Biscotti:

- 2 ½ cups all-purpose flour
- 1 cup granulated sugar
- 1 teaspoon baking powder
- ¼ teaspoon salt
- ¼ cup unsalted butter, melted
- 3 large eggs
- 1 tablespoon grated orange zest (about 1 large orange)
- 1 teaspoon vanilla extract
- 1 cup sliced almonds (toasted if desired)

For Glazing (Optional):

- 1 cup powdered sugar
- 2-3 tablespoons fresh orange juice

Instructions:

1. **Preheat Oven:**
   - Preheat your oven to 350°F (175°C).
   - Line a baking sheet with parchment paper.
2. **Prepare the Biscotti Dough:**
   - In a large bowl, whisk together the flour, granulated sugar, baking powder, and salt.
   - In another bowl, combine the melted butter, eggs, grated orange zest, and vanilla extract.
   - Add the wet ingredients to the dry ingredients and mix until just combined.
   - Fold in the sliced almonds.
3. **Shape and Bake:**
   - Divide the dough in half and shape each half into a log about 12 inches long and 2 inches wide on the prepared baking sheet.
   - Bake for 25-30 minutes, or until the logs are golden brown and firm to the touch.
4. **Cool and Slice:**
   - Remove the logs from the oven and let them cool on the baking sheet for about 10 minutes.
   - Reduce the oven temperature to 300°F (150°C).
   - Transfer the logs to a cutting board and slice them diagonally into ½-inch wide slices using a serrated knife.
   - Place the slices cut-side down on the baking sheet.
5. **Bake Again:**
   - Return the biscotti to the oven and bake for an additional 15-20 minutes, or until they are dry and crisp.

- Let the biscotti cool completely on a wire rack.
6. **Prepare the Glaze (Optional):**
    - In a small bowl, whisk together the powdered sugar and orange juice until smooth.
    - Drizzle the glaze over the cooled biscotti, allowing it to set before serving.
7. **Serve:**
    - Enjoy your Orange Almond Biscotti with a cup of coffee or tea. They're perfect for dipping and make a wonderful treat for any time of day.

These Orange Almond Biscotti have a delightful crunch and a lovely combination of citrus and nutty flavors. They store well in an airtight container, making them great for making ahead and enjoying throughout the week!

Caramel Apple Cake

Ingredients:

For the Cake:

- 2 ½ cups all-purpose flour
- 1 ½ teaspoons baking powder
- ½ teaspoon baking soda
- ½ teaspoon salt
- 1 teaspoon ground cinnamon
- ¼ teaspoon ground nutmeg
- ½ cup (1 stick) unsalted butter, softened
- 1 cup granulated sugar
- ½ cup packed brown sugar
- 2 large eggs
- 1 cup sour cream
- 1 teaspoon vanilla extract
- 2 cups peeled, cored, and diced apples (such as Granny Smith or Honeycrisp)

For the Caramel Sauce:

- 1 cup granulated sugar
- 6 tablespoons unsalted butter
- ¼ cup heavy cream
- 1 teaspoon vanilla extract
- Pinch of salt

For the Glaze (Optional):

- 1 cup powdered sugar
- 2-3 tablespoons milk (or heavy cream)
- ¼ teaspoon vanilla extract

Optional Garnish:

- Whipped cream
- Additional diced apples

Instructions:

1. **Preheat Oven:**
    - Preheat your oven to 350°F (175°C).
    - Grease and flour a 9x13-inch baking pan or line it with parchment paper.
2. **Prepare the Cake Batter:**
    - In a medium bowl, whisk together the flour, baking powder, baking soda, salt, cinnamon, and nutmeg. Set aside.

- In a large bowl, cream together the softened butter, granulated sugar, and brown sugar until light and fluffy.
- Beat in the eggs one at a time, mixing well after each addition.
- Mix in the sour cream and vanilla extract until smooth.
- Gradually add the dry ingredients to the wet ingredients, mixing until just combined.
- Fold in the diced apples.

3. **Bake the Cake:**
    - Pour the batter into the prepared baking pan and smooth the top with a spatula.
    - Bake for 35-40 minutes, or until a toothpick inserted into the center comes out clean and the cake is golden brown.

4. **Prepare the Caramel Sauce:**
    - In a medium saucepan, heat the granulated sugar over medium heat, stirring constantly until it melts and turns a deep amber color.
    - Carefully add the butter and stir until melted and combined.
    - Slowly add the heavy cream, stirring continuously until smooth. Be cautious as the mixture will bubble up.
    - Stir in the vanilla extract and a pinch of salt.
    - Allow the caramel sauce to cool slightly before using.

5. **Glaze the Cake (Optional):**
    - In a small bowl, whisk together the powdered sugar, milk (or cream), and vanilla extract until smooth and pourable.
    - Drizzle the glaze over the cooled cake.

6. **Serve:**
    - Drizzle the caramel sauce over the cake, allowing some to pool around the edges.
    - Garnish with whipped cream and additional diced apples if desired.

This Caramel Apple Cake is a rich, flavorful dessert with a tender crumb and delicious caramel topping. It's perfect for fall and winter, or any time you want to enjoy a comforting and indulgent treat!

Strawberry Lemonade Bars

Ingredients:

For the Crust:

- 1 ½ cups all-purpose flour
- ¼ cup granulated sugar
- ¼ teaspoon salt
- ½ cup (1 stick) unsalted butter, cold and cut into small pieces

For the Filling:

- 1 cup granulated sugar
- 2 large eggs
- ⅓ cup fresh lemon juice (about 2 lemons)
- 1 tablespoon lemon zest (about 1 lemon)
- ¼ cup all-purpose flour
- ½ cup finely chopped fresh strawberries (or use frozen strawberries, thawed and drained)

For the Glaze (Optional):

- 1 cup powdered sugar
- 2-3 tablespoons fresh lemon juice
- 1 tablespoon finely chopped fresh strawberries

Instructions:

1. **Preheat Oven:**
   - Preheat your oven to 350°F (175°C).
   - Line an 8x8-inch baking pan with parchment paper, leaving an overhang for easy removal.
2. **Prepare the Crust:**
   - In a medium bowl, whisk together the flour, granulated sugar, and salt.
   - Cut in the cold butter using a pastry cutter or your fingers until the mixture resembles coarse crumbs.
   - Press the mixture firmly into the bottom of the prepared pan to form an even layer.
3. **Bake the Crust:**
   - Bake the crust for 15-20 minutes, or until it is lightly golden brown. Remove from the oven and set aside.
4. **Prepare the Filling:**
   - In a large bowl, whisk together the granulated sugar, eggs, lemon juice, and lemon zest until well combined.
   - Stir in the flour until smooth.
   - Fold in the chopped strawberries.
5. **Assemble and Bake:**

- Pour the filling over the pre-baked crust and spread it evenly with a spatula.
- Bake for 25-30 minutes, or until the filling is set and the edges are slightly golden. The center should still be slightly jiggly.

6. **Cool:**
    - Allow the bars to cool completely in the pan on a wire rack.
    - Once cooled, refrigerate for at least 2 hours to set properly.
7. **Prepare the Glaze (Optional):**
    - In a small bowl, whisk together the powdered sugar and lemon juice until smooth. Adjust the consistency with more lemon juice if necessary.
    - Stir in the finely chopped fresh strawberries.
8. **Glaze and Serve:**
    - Once the bars are chilled, spread or drizzle the glaze over the top.
    - Cut into squares and serve.

These Strawberry Lemonade Bars are wonderfully tangy and sweet, with a perfect balance of flavors and a delightful texture. They are sure to be a hit at any gathering or as a refreshing treat on a warm day!

Bourbon Pecan Pie

Ingredients:

For the Pie Crust:

- 1 ½ cups all-purpose flour
- ¼ teaspoon salt
- ¼ cup granulated sugar
- ½ cup (1 stick) unsalted butter, cold and cut into small cubes
- 1 large egg yolk
- 2-3 tablespoons ice water

For the Filling:

- 1 cup light corn syrup
- 1 cup packed brown sugar
- ¼ cup unsalted butter, melted
- 4 large eggs
- ¼ cup bourbon
- 1 teaspoon vanilla extract
- 2 cups pecan halves

Optional Garnish:

- Whipped cream
- Additional pecan halves

Instructions:

1. **Prepare the Pie Crust:**
   - In a large bowl, whisk together the flour, salt, and granulated sugar.
   - Cut in the cold butter using a pastry cutter or your fingers until the mixture resembles coarse crumbs.
   - In a small bowl, whisk together the egg yolk and 2 tablespoons of ice water.
   - Add the egg mixture to the flour mixture and stir until just combined. Add an additional tablespoon of ice water if needed.
   - Gather the dough into a ball, wrap it in plastic wrap, and refrigerate for at least 30 minutes.
2. **Preheat Oven:**
   - Preheat your oven to 350°F (175°C).
3. **Roll Out and Fit the Crust:**
   - On a lightly floured surface, roll out the chilled dough to fit a 9-inch pie dish.
   - Transfer the dough to the pie dish, trimming any excess and crimping the edges as desired.
   - Line the crust with parchment paper or aluminum foil and fill with pie weights or dried beans.

       - Bake the crust for 10 minutes, then remove the weights and parchment/foil. Bake for an additional 5 minutes until the crust is lightly golden. Set aside.
4. **Prepare the Filling:**
    - In a large bowl, whisk together the corn syrup, brown sugar, melted butter, eggs, bourbon, and vanilla extract until smooth and well combined.
    - Stir in the pecan halves.
5. **Assemble and Bake:**
    - Pour the pecan filling into the pre-baked pie crust.
    - Bake for 50-60 minutes, or until the filling is set and the top is golden brown. The center may still jiggle slightly but should not be liquid.
    - If the edges of the crust start to over-brown, cover them with aluminum foil during the last 15-20 minutes of baking.
6. **Cool:**
    - Allow the pie to cool completely on a wire rack before slicing. The filling will firm up as it cools.
7. **Serve:**
    - Serve the Bourbon Pecan Pie at room temperature or slightly warmed.
    - Garnish with whipped cream and additional pecan halves if desired.

This Bourbon Pecan Pie is a decadent dessert with a rich, nutty flavor and a hint of bourbon that adds a sophisticated touch. It's perfect for holiday gatherings, special occasions, or as a treat to enjoy with family and friends!